P9-EGM-670

FROM THE EDITORS OF KNITTER'S MAGAZINE

a unique
and elegant
approach to
your yarn
collection

SALLY
MELVILLE
styles

PHOTOGRAPHY
Alexis Xenakis

author
Sally Melville

photographer
Alexis Xenakis

editor
Elaine Rowley

BOOKS

AN XRX BOOK

PUBLISHER
Alexis Yiorgos Xenakis

EDITOR
Elaine Rowley

KNITTING EDITOR
Ann Regis

FASHION DIRECTOR
Nancy J. Thomas

PHOTOGRAPHER
Alexis Yiorgos Xenakis

DIRECTOR, PUBLISHING SERVICES
David Xenakis

GRAPHIC DESIGNER
Bob Natz

COVER DESIGNER
Mark Sampson

BOOK PRODUCTION MANAGER
Debbie Gage

DIGITAL COLOR SPECIALIST
Daren Morgan

PRODUCTION
Jay Reeve
Lynda Selle
Carol Skallerud

MARKETING DIRECTOR
Tad Anderson

MIS
Benjamin Xenakis

FIRST PUBLISHED IN USA IN 1998 BY XRX, INC.
PO BOX 1525, SIOUX FALLS, SD 57101-1525

LIBRARY OF CONGRESS
CATALOG CARD NUMBER: 98-90712

ISBN 0-9646391-4-9

Produced in Sioux Falls, South Dakota, by XRX, Inc., 605.338.2450

Color separations by Digital Imaging, Sioux Falls, SD

Printed in Hong Kong

BOOKS

Foreword

Knitting is a metaphor for life. Everything that life offers, so too does knitting. There are the plans made, some of which inevitably unravel. Crimson leaves, golden sunsets, and the verdant green of the deep forest are all reflected in the knitter's hands. The glimpse of beauty seen, the vision of perfect beauty pursued: each are the hallmark of those who would leave a legacy to the world. There are the supple soft textures of a knitted garment, sensual to the touch and speaking of other possibilities. New beginnings invite us forward, even as disappointment lurks should our technique or imagination fail. But who among knitters has not felt the frustration of a difficult task give way to the satisfaction of accomplishment, the common experience of all who strive?

Knitting and life merge when a knitted work is given to another: the smile, the embrace, and the warmth of human relationships.

Sally Melville has given her readers a powerful tool to advance their art. It is based on what should be a guiding principle of our age: waste not. Yet it does not compromise on either artistic scope or excellence of design. Using those materials on hand serves only to invite more ingenuity of design. From scraps and remnants, a knitted garment of intricate beauty can arise; what was once rejected as of little consequence can become a work of lasting meaning. This, too, is a lesson for life.

While the approach of this book echoes the frugality of the past, its readers are offered the means to create new and innovative work. Knitting is, of course, an ancient technique, and we value this link to the uncounted generations that have preceded us. But knitting should not be content to merely repeat the designs and forms of the past, familiar and comfortable though they are. Like any practiced art, knitting needs to move forward, endlessly exploring new avenues of expression. Imagination, disciplined by the characteristics of the materials, calls forth a practical solution, experimenting until it does.

Let the knitter demonstrate to the watching child how accomplishment is summoned from a mass of raw ingredients. Speak to the child of persistence and concentration, of colors seen and textures felt. Let the child see the joy of a work in progress.

Recognizing that any work of excellence requires preparation, planning, and attention to detail, Sally Melville guides the reader through each essential step. While there are no instant answers in the world of craft and art, these suggestions and recommendations are both straightforward and precise. Applied meticulously, they will result in garments of startling beauty and exceptional variety. Equally important, they significantly extend the knitter's range and capability, hinting at the creation of unique and ever more personal designs.

But it must be recognized that while this book can provide sure and expert guidance, can invite and encourage the knitter to enter a new and exciting realm of endeavor, it cannot replace the motivation to create. It cannot replace the commitment to proceed or the determination to complete. It cannot replace the knitter's passion. That comes from the heart.

Larry Smith
Department of Economics,
University of Waterloo

I first learned the importance of creativity from Larry Smith, and it changed how I saw the world. Problems were good things, because they led to problem solving—the basis of all creativity. Failures were never failures but opportunities to learn. They taught me most of what I know about knitting and the nature of life!

—Sally Melville

XRX Books would like to hear from you!

We can't publish all the knitting books in the world—only the finest.

We are knitting enthusiasts and book lovers. Our mission is simple: to produce quality books that showcase the beauty of the knitting and give our readers inspiration, confidence, and skill-building instructions.

Publishing begins as a partnership between author and publisher. XRX Books attracts the best authors and designers in the knitting universe because we share their passion for excellence. But books also require a shared vision: photographer Alexis Xenakis and his team bring the garments and fabrics to glorious life. This is where our journey begins.

Cutting-edge computer technology allows us to focus on editing and designing our publications. XRX Books editor Elaine Rowley can exchange files from South Dakota with our knitting editor in New York or our authors, wherever they happen to live, within a matter of minutes. Our digital consultant, David Xenakis, and his team insure accuracy of color and texture in our images. Graphic artist Bob Natz, believing that design is not good unless it functions well, produces beautiful, easy-to-read pages.

Now those pages are in your hands and your journey begins.

Tell us what you think:

- **by mail**
  XRX Books
  PO Box 1525
  Sioux Falls, South Dakota
  57101-1525

- **by phone**
  605-338-2450

- **by e-mail**
  rowley.elaine@xrx-inc.com

- **by fax**
  605-338-2994

- **on xrx-inc.com**
  You may visit our XRX Books site on the World Wide Web: xrx-inc.com

- **On our Knitter's OnLine forums:**
  Join the conversation and post your reactions and comments in our book discussion bulletin boards: xrx-inc.com/scripts/webx.dll?knitalk

We look forward to hearing from you. New journeys are under way.

——In memory of my husband Ken and of my grandmother "Honey."

ACKNOWLEDGEMENTS

First and foremost, thanks to the incomparably competent crew at XRX for making me a beautiful book. Special thanks go to Alexis Xenakis, for his energy and for his talent with a camera, and to Elaine Rowley, for her vision, patience, kindness, and ability to read my writing.

Only two-thirds of the garments for this book were knit by me. The others were knit by extra-ordinary knitters whom I am most grateful to know: Stasia Bania and Lynn Philips.

Additional thanks go to the following: Nancy J. Thomas (for directing me to Elaine Rowley), David Xenakis (for seeing beautiful fabrics), Ann Regis (for articulating what this book is really about), Sandi Minnes (and her family—Dave, Kevin, and Jonathan—for modeling and for making our photo shoot such a pleasure), Bjanka Dragicevic (a wonderful first-time model), Sharon Airhart (for her amazing overnight editing of the initial chapters), Dawna Rowlson (for the morning mail), Joan Pequegnat (who kept me knitting), Jill Officer (for trying overdyeing first), Ann Budd and Hope Castle (for telling me to continue), Gudrun Wilkin of Elizabeth's Wool Shop in Kitchener, Ontario (who knows what I need before I do), Barbara Klunker (for inspiring me), the Kitchener-Waterloo Knitters' Guild (for the community it provides), and all my students in all my classes (who have taught me so much!).

Three—all knitters!—special people deserve mention for their love, support, and companionship: Laurel Thom, Mel Biggs, and Nancy (Melville) Hodgetts.

I am especially pleased to offer this book to my knitting mentor—Lee Andersen—in return for her encouragement and sisterhood.

Finally, this is for my children: Jeremy and Caddy, you are a joy to know, and you bless my life.

Sally

Contents

First Considerations

Good ol' Garter

Simple Fairisle

Not-Your-Usual Intarsia

Sally Melville *styles*

Introduction

Five years ago, I began

what I thought was a

book about working

through a yarn "stash"—

about projects and

techniques that knitters

could use to work through

their piles, bags,

baskets of leftovers.

It has long seemed to me that other crafts have rather elegant techniques for the use of leftovers. Crocheting has granny squares, and my English grandmother's afghan in this technique is one of my family's prized possessions. Patchwork quilting was originally built on the use of scraps, so the treasured family favorites of my American in-laws include familiar bits of fabric from earlier days. Knitting, however, has no such long-standing tradition of using leftovers to make beautiful new projects.

And, yes, most knitters have a stash—a closet, a dresser, a guest room, even a freezer full of yarn! What they don't have is a way to make sense of it all, a way to turn balls of this and that into fabrics as lovely—and projects as classic—as those precious quilts and afghans.

That might be because working with different yarns of a stash is difficult! Different colors, different yardages, different weights, different fibers; a little of this, a lot of that. What pattern will make good use of such variety? Which goes with what? Will I have enough?

As I set about solving these problems, I discovered that sometimes what I most needed to do—to make the stash yarns come together and produce a beautiful fabric—was to go to the yarn shop and *buy more yarn!* I sometimes needed more of a color than I had on hand. Or I needed more variety in texture to make the fabric exciting. Or I needed a unifying main color to pull the contrast colors together.

By developing new techniques, I was modifying the old adage "You have to spend money to make money." My own little axiom became "It takes a little cash to use up a lotta stash!"

Then something quite different began to happen. I walked into yarn shops and bought one ball of anything that struck my fancy! I was, after all, developing techniques for putting together different weights, fibers, and colors, so I could be quite self-indulgent. To buy a yarn, I no longer needed to know what pattern I would use and how much I might need: I could just buy without much thought and certainly without guilt! That's when I began to see this book from an expanded perspective, one well beyond leftovers.

Perhaps the real work of this book is to foster a knitter's artistry and creativity. At least, it could give knitters—both novice and experienced—the opportunity to depart from traditional patterns. At best, this book might provide inspiration for knitters to create their own new ways of working. More, it might help all knitters look at yarns in a new way and have even more fun in their favorite shops.

It is my hope that wherever you are in your knitting, this book will help you add to and work through your collection— of yarn, skills, artistry, and reasons to find joy in knitting.

What do you have to work with?

HOW TO ARRANGE YOUR YARN COLLECTION

There are various ways to arrange a yarn collection, and I think I have tried them all!

Like most knitters, I began with the "bag it, find a drawer, squeeze it in" method of dealing with my stash.

Once I actually started putting some thought and work into arranging my yarn, the organizing principle that seemed most logical was to arrange yarns by their weight and fiber. That meant grouping all fine wools, or medium-weight mohairs, or heavy cottons, or thin metallics, each in their own container.

This proved to be not very efficient; in fact, as long as my yarns were organized in this way, I never made much use of them. The system made it difficult to put together color combinations because it trapped me into seeing and using only yarns of the same weight and fiber.

A snapshot of part of Sally's stash arranged by color and in plastic bins.

I then tried storing yarn in a way that seemed least logical but turned out to be most productive. Instead of arranging by fiber or weight, I began arranging my yarn by color.

When I arranged by color—all my blue-greens, or dark reds, or clear whites in their own bins—I paid no attention to fiber content or to weight. When I pulled down the bins and began combining colors for a "leftovers" garment, I only chose yarn weights and fibers that would work together.

If you choose this "color" method, I recommend first picking out your multiples—more than three balls

of the same yarn in the same dye lot. On a piece of masking tape, write the number of balls. Stick the tape on one ball, and relegate the rest to longer-term storage—the guest room, the attic, or, like my godmother, the freezer! Add the marked ball to your yarn stash. Here it will represent the stored quantity without taking up unnecessary space in your stash arrangement.

Arrange the rest of your yarns by color, using the rainbow or spectrum as a guide. Put your yarn into piles of blues, purples, reds, oranges, yellows, greens. Make additional piles of blacks, whites, grays, browns, metallics, and variegateds. You will likely end up with piles of different sizes.

At this point you need to think about the containment of your stash. Where are all these piles of yarn going to go? I use clear, plastic containers. They are light, readily available, reasonably inexpensive, and they allow me to see the contents. The sizes I use are all 5½" deep, so my balls and half-balls can't get too deeply buried, and their other dimensions are 16 X 23" and 16 X 11".

Does each of your rainbow-colored piles fit into a container? If so, your job is done! If not, you need to divide your piles further. The next subdivision may be according to intensity: lights versus mediums versus darks. If some of your piles are still too large for your containers, try dividing them by hue: yellow-green versus green versus blue-green (look at the color wheel on p. 13 for guidance).

If you use the containers I do and have the space and inclination, you can build shelving just over 5½" tall—so you don't have to use the lids—and 16" deep. The shelves should be 46" wide to accommodate two 23" bins or four 11" bins.

When finished, your yarns should be displayed in a beautiful, inviting, spectral array!

HOW TO KNOW IF YOU HAVE ENOUGH

A serious consideration when working with the variety of yarns in your collection is how to know if you have enough.

For the patterns that follow, we have offered yarn amounts in terms of yardage as well as numbers of full balls. In addition, the following guidelines and principles should help you estimate if you have enough yarn for a row, an area, or a project.

◆ To work a single row or area of one-color stockinette stitch requires three times the width of the row or area, plus an allowance for the tails to be woven in.

The shortest distance from **A** to **B** is a straight line:

B ──────────────────────────── A

When you knit, the yarn does not travel in a straight line:

B ⌇⌇⌇⌇⌇⌇⌇⌇⌇⌇⌇ A

So, knitting from **A** to **B** uses a length of yarn approximately three times the distance from **A** to **B.**

B ════════════════════════
   ════════════════════════ A

◆ To work a single row of fairisle in which the two colors are distributed more or less equally requires twice the width of the row in each color, plus an allowance for the tails to be woven in.

◆ If you are working with some kind of regular, repeating shape or motif, rip out your tension swatch and measure the length used for the motif. Topher's Pullover (p. 72) worked in Tweed stitch squares is an example of a garment worked in a regular, repeating motif. For this and similar patterns, we have already measured the length needed for each motif.

◆ If none of the above applies, try working randomly, changing colors as you wish! Tricia's Coat (p. 111) is an example of a garment in which the contrast colors are changed randomly.

◆ If you are working with a yarn as main color and are worried about having enough, it helps if this color is dark (charcoal gray, navy, black) so if you have to switch to another yarn it won't be noticeable.

◆ If you want a dark or main color but don't have enough in that color, choose a variety of yarns with the same fiber content (100% wool or cotton) and give them a dye bath in that dark main color.

◆ Remember that ribbing and other edgings can eat up a lot of yarn, and they really don't have to be done in the same yarn as the main color. Work these ribbings and edgings in alternate yarns or in a combination of yarns, or begin your piece with a provisional cast-on that can be ripped out so you can work your ribbings later and in whatever yarn you have enough of.

◆ If you are using one yarn as the main color in the body and another in the edging, use the better yarn for the edgings. Its quality will be more obvious because it is standing alone.

◆ If you run out of a dye lot, blend some of it with a new dye lot by working two rows in each for an inch or so. In this book, however, dye lots rarely matter.

How do you combine colors?

When I teach design, or when I work on a design, I think of the knit fabric in terms of its three components: yarn, color, and stitch pattern. Then I think in terms of which of these is going to remain the same and which is going to be changed. Some very successful garments are made in a single yarn, color, and stitch pattern. But that's not what working with a yarn collection is about.

In any given project, knitters may work with change of color (intarsia or fairisle) or with change of texture (varied stitches) but almost always use just one kind of yarn. Using a yarn collection to create beautiful knitting means learning to combine different yarns—different colors, weights, and fibers.

WORK WITH THE PRINCIPLES OF COLOR THEORY

In this chapter, I discuss color, laying out simple suggestions for working with change of color to produce beautiful fabrics. In some of the garments for the book, I have wandered outside these guidelines. You may do the same thing! But having a good handle on these basic principles allows us to depart from them with considered thought and confidence.

Use a main color, preferably darker than your contrast colors

When you are working with a variety of fibers and colors, a main color helps the work look less scrappy. It serves as a unifying element drawing together all the contrasting yarns and colors you choose. (By the way, in knitting terminology "contrasting color" does not necessarily mean color in great contrast to another. Contrasting color simply means yarn other than the main color.)

Once, while speaking at a knitting conference, I wore my Kilim Coat Dress (p. 125) as an illustration of the work we would do in my class. Later, I learned that a woman in the audience had said, "Well, that's fine for Sally who has lovely leftovers, but mine are a 'dog from every town!'" How I longed to meet her. First, I'd congratulate her on her wonderful turn of phrase. Second, I'd show her that my coat dress was, indeed, "a dog from every town." She didn't know it because I had used a single, main color to tie all of those "dogs" together.

Also, we have two kinds of yarn in our collection: multiple balls of something for which we never found the right project, and single balls of this and that. Using multiple balls of a main color means finding a purpose for the "what-do-I-do-with-this" yarn.

In some of the garments in this book, the use of a main color is not obvious. Many people, when first looking at Topher's Pullover (p. 74), are astounded to hear that two of every four rows are worked in a charcoal gray tweed. The main yarn is itself not apparent, but it subtly blends the contrast colors together, and its use makes all the difference in the finished product.

And sometimes, two "main" colors can be used to draw together a large number of other colors. In Tricia's Coat (p. 111) there are two unifying colors used: one is the dark blue through which the randomly-changed contrast colors are woven, and the second is the navy blue, woven in diagonal lines to separate the contrast colors. The use of this second unifying color brings order to the random nature of the color work and makes the garment look less like "odd-ball" knitting.

A background color integrates the other yarns and colors.

Garter squares worked in a variety of fibers and colors can look "scrappy."

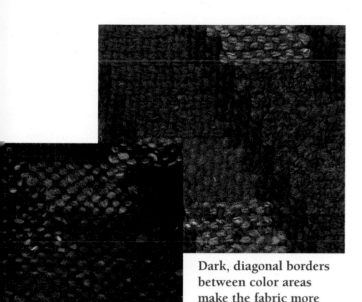

Dark, diagonal borders between color areas make the fabric more attractive.

Random changes of yarn can ...ack order.

When choosing a main color, I prefer the look produced by working with a color darker than the contrast colors. This preference is so strong that not a single garment in this book has a lighter main color. Even the very pale Annalee's Jacket with Round Neck (p. 101) uses a darker off-white than the others in the garment. The only garment that comes even close to ignoring this preference is the Ski Suit Cardigan (p. 85): here the main color is lighter than only a couple of the contrast colors and is the same intensity as most.

Your preference may not be mine. See the accompanying swatches and make your own decision.

A difference in background color is significant. I prefer using a background color that is darker than the other colors.

. . . with a dark background.

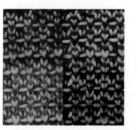

The same colors worked with a light background.

. . . with a medium background.

Stay within a tonal range for your contrast colors

Either before or after choosing your main color, you will choose the contrast colors for the project. Staying within a tonal range is the simplest and safest way to choose these colors.

If you look at the accompanying color wheel, you will see concentric rings. The inner rings are quite pale; the rings are brighter and more intense toward the middle of the wheel; the outer rings are darker. Each of these rings is known as a "tonal range." Colors in the same tonal range generally work well together. This is the first principle I would recommend: stay within a tonal range, working more or less with all lights, or all brights (mediums), or all darks.

I do say "more or less," because some of the yarns you choose will not be accurately depicted on the color wheel and some won't appear on the color wheel at all.

Colors that do not appear on the color wheel are what I call "dusties" because they have gray undertones. These colors comprise their own tonal range and look quite good together. But they don't look good in combination with clear, bright colors.

When you're choosing colors, you might also consider fiber, because fiber content has an impact on how a color appears. Cottons are dyed over a clear white, so their colors are quite crisp and bright. Wools are dyed over a creamier base, so their colors have warmer under-

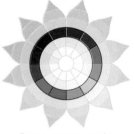

From center to outside:
1st ring	light intensity
2nd ring	light-medium intensity
3rd ring	**medium intensity**
4th ring	medium-dark intensity
5th ring	dark intensity
6th ring	darkest intensity

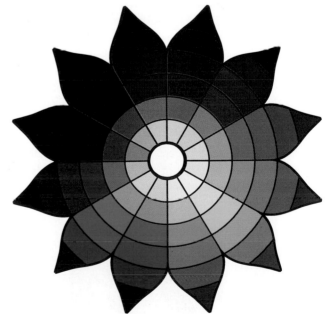

Each ring of the color wheel is a "tonal range" and the colors within a ring generally work well together. The caption under the small wheel explains the terminology used throughout this book.

FOCAL POINTS

A single spot out of tonal range will produce a focal point. Depending upon placement, this can be a feature or a disaster. Two focal points are difficult because . . . well . . . we want to avoid "headlights" and issues of symmetry. Three or more diminishes the impact enough to make the color work. For some pithy advice on the issue, I quote Lee Andersen: "Once is a mistake, twice is a problem, three times is a design."

tones. Most acrylic yarns start as a liquid that is dyed and then spun. The colors tend to be either flatter or brighter than the colors produced by dyeing a natural product. Here again, the use of a main color eases the differences between colors when the fibers are different, but you might watch for glaring variations in tonal quality.

One bright rust square was deliberately put onto the back of Laurel's Jacket to illustrate that a color out of range does not work.

To see if your colors are in the same tonal range, try putting them into a pile and squinting. If one of them is too light, too bright, or too dark, it should be obvious.

Or you can try this trick recommended by Lee Anderson, of Columbia, Maryland. Put all of the yarns onto a black and white photocopier and make a photocopy. By reducing your yarns to black and white, you can more easily judge the lightness and darkness.

The Kilim Coat Dress depends on the interplay of light, medium, and dark colors.

What exactly are you looking for? You are looking for a combination that does not have any singularly obvious light or bright or dark yarns. The inclusion of any one of these would mean you have moved out of your tonal range to produce a focal point. Focal points are okay as long as we are careful where we put them, or as long as we feature enough of them that their effect is diluted.

The strongest focal point is produced by including a yarn that is brighter than the rest. Look at the accompanying photo of the back of Laurel's Jacket (from p. 65). The colors chosen are mostly dark, but some are light, and all are kind of dusty. The inclusion of one rich, bright orange-red square is quite out of place!

Sometimes we need to step out of a tonal range to make a color pattern work. For example, the Kilim Coat Dress depends on an interplay of light to medium to dark in the contrast colors used. However, notice that the lights are used for the smallest areas. This is usually the best choice for light yarns because they are most demanding of the eye's attention. The darks (in the outside spaces) are used in the largest areas because they are least demanding of the eye's attention.

Staying within a tonal range is a good, safe guideline to follow, but it is not one that is meant to be applied slavishly.

Stick to a third or a half of the color wheel for your contrast colors

Even when we stay close to a tonal range, we might wish to further reduce our choices. Although the temptation may be to use as many colors as possible—to use as much of our yarn collection as possible—covering the entire color wheel is not necessary and perhaps not even desirable. Working with a third or a half of the wheel usually produces more successful color combinations.

Choosing all warm colors or all cool colors is the most common way to work with half of the color spectrum. Look at the accompanying color wheel: the warm colors are on the right half—from reds to yellow-greens; the cool colors are on the left half—from purple-reds to greens.

Shannon's Pullover covers the entire spectrum.

You can limit your choices to any third or half of the wheel. Try the bottom half (as I did for the worsted-weight version of Topher's Pullover on p. 77), or the top half, or split the wheel on the diagonal. Any split can produce color combinations that work.

You can also work with an even smaller portion of the color wheel. If you love and have lots of blue, go ahead and make an all-blue garment. I had lots of beiges, off-whites, taupes, and light to medium browns, until I made the subtly colored Uncle Jeremy's Vest (p. 34). There are other garments in this book that use an even narrower range of color: the all-gray Gander "Blips" Vest (p. 35), and most of the designs in the Tweed Stitch with Cables section (p. 88–101).

I designed two garments for this book whose contrast colors cover the entire spectrum: Jessica's Jacket (p. 28) and Shannon's Pullover (p. 110). I do think that if working with the entire spectrum, it helps to order the contrast colors just as they are on the color wheel, rather than randomly mixing them.

In both of these garments, the contrast colors are from the middle intensity range of the color wheel (fairly bright stuff), and the main color is black. It would be entirely possible to produce either garment with the contrast colors from a lighter range. To complement this softness, you might choose a light neutral for the main color.

When selecting complementary colors to use in a project, work with the color wheel.

Use a color complementary to your contrast colors

Complementary colors are those that lie directly opposite each other on the color wheel: red/green, blue/orange, yellow/purple. Our eyes actually want to see these complementary colors—in effect to complete the color wheel—so the inclusion of one can give a kind of balance to colors in combination.

When we work with a range of contrast colors, as we will likely do when working from our yarn collection, how do we find its complement? Look at the area of the color wheel that represents your color choices. Go to the middle of this area, and then look directly opposite. This is your single complementary color. If you like the look, add a bit of it (see Topher's Pullover, p. 73 and Laurel's Jacket, p. 67). Alternatively, don't use this color but use the colors on either side of it. This is a split complementary, and it also works well.

One note of caution: You may notice from looking at the color wheel that your eye is drawn to the warm colors and away from the cooler ones. This means that if you make a garment with warm colors and include a cool-colored complementary, the cool color is not going to draw the eye's attention. But if you make a garment with cool colors and include a warm-colored complementary, the warm color is going to draw the eye's attention and produce a focal point. (As close as I ever get to a warm color in a cool-colored garment is to use a yellow-green. I like the way this color looks in almost any color combination. See Tricia's Coat on p. 111.)

MATCHING COLORS
If you are trying to match the color in a garment, but cannot find quite that color in yarn, use the colors that appear each side of it on the color wheel. If appropriate, twist them together to produce the color you want. Or, simply use each in the garment to produce the illusion of using the color you were trying to match.

Warm side

Cool side

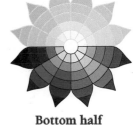

Bottom half

Red/green

CHOOSING COLORS
When we are young, we have very high color, but as we get older, we lose color—from our hair, our skin, and our eyes. Choosing the right colors for our skin tones becomes more important as we age so we can maximize what little there is left!

TRY OTHER "COLOR-DEAF" POSSIBILITIES

Elaine Rowley, my editor, first introduced me to this expression. It perfectly describes people who can be told all the color theory in the world but can't "hear" it in a way that translates to the visual. The options that follow are for them. These methods are more informal and are about "seeing" colors more than about "hearing" theory. But they are also methods that even the most color-aware knitters can enjoy.

Work from something you like

You can produce color combinations that will work if you find something that uses colors you like and gather your own yarns to mimic its color choices, paying attention to proportion as well as color. (For the Kilim Coat Dress, I used the color combinations in a Paul Klee painting, "Ancient Sound Abstract on Black," gathering my yarns into piles that covered the color range he used and in the same proportion.)

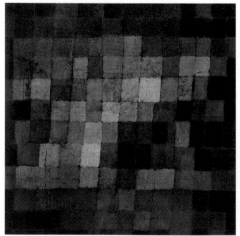

A favorite painting provided color choices and proportions for the Kilim Coat Dress.

Closeup of the Kilim Coat Dress.

Pick a color you like . . .
and use anything you can stand next to it. . .
then use them all in a small, repeating color pattern

There is not much discipline involved in saying "Choose a color and anything you can stand next to it."

This alone is not likely to inspire confidence. But I did exactly this for two garments in the book, so perhaps here the best instruction is by example.

For the child's version of Caddy's Cardigan on p. 50, I began with the strong yellow-green—one of my favorite colors—and included everything that I liked sitting beside it. I was very, *very* picky, carefully considering each color before including it.

Caddy's Cardigan (child's version)

For the adult's version in the same section, I went to a fabulous yarn shop and chose greens, blues, and purples and every tweedy or variegated yarn that had any green, blue, or purple in it. I had begun with color choices from a very limited portion of the color wheel, so the inclusion of yarns with small blips of color from other parts of the wheel would only make the final effect more interesting.

Caddy's Cardigan (adult's version)

The yarn you begin with may be a variegated one. If so, avoid a mistake often made when matching anything to variegated yarns. This mistake is to hold the variegated yarn *too close* while looking to match it or while considering it in combination with something else. The colors that are in the variegated yarn when it is looked at from close range may not actually be there—or match it at all—when looked at from a little distance.

Why does this happen? Why does the combination look wonderful at 12" but truly awful from farther away? Because at a distance, the eye cannot discern the yarn's small bits of color, so it blends them. It now "sees" only these blended colors. What matches the variegated yarn will be these blended colors. (And so what matches the variegated yarn from a distance may not appear in it at all when seen at close range!) How to sort this out? Look at a variegated yarn from a few feet, then go looking for the colors you see from this range.

Once you've chosen your colors, what appears before you may seem a rather undisciplined lot. But using them in a small color pattern repeat will ensure that this combination works. Again, both the garments in the Simple Fairisle section were worked this way: take a look at the charts on p. 47 to see what is meant by a small color pattern repeat.

To understand why this works, think of a kaleidoscope: small pieces of colored glass which might not look wonderful together produce a spectacular pattern and combination when fractured and repeated. There is an instrument—often sold as a child's toy in up-scale toy stores or in art gallery gift shops—known as a "teleidoscope." It works like a kaleidoscope except that it has no colored glass, only a fractured lens which takes whatever it is looking at and repeats it. It's a wonderful tool for looking at a pile of yarn and seeing what a small, frequently-repeating color pattern will look like.

As you look at your pile through the teleidoscope, move it to see other proportions. Add a color, remove a color, or change the placement of a color—all as you look through the tool—to see even more possibilities.

Use the garment patterns from this book

If you lack confidence in your ability to combine colors, you've probably been following patterns all your life and are happy to continue to do so! But what are you going to do with a book that does not give yarn brands and color numbers?

Each of the patterns that follows has a set of Color Principles in which the colors chosen for the garment are described in two ways. First of all, the main and contrast colors used are described in words—in terms of intensity (light or medium or dark) and also in terms of colors on the color wheel (red-purple or purple or blue-green). In addition, the color wheel is shown beside these written descriptions with the colors used in the garment shown

to full intensity and with those not used "ghosted" out.

So to work with this book, go to your stash or your yarn shop and pick colors that come as close as possible to what is shown to full intensity. Remember that a color wheel is a simplified tool, so you will never match all colors exactly. "Purple" would be anything you would put in your purple bin of yarn. Get as close as you can, then go play!

What if you like the garment but not the colors I used? Look at the full intensity colors shown and compare them to the full color wheel on p. 140. Imagine rotating the pattern of colors I used around the color wheel until it sits on colors you like. Do you like this better? Almost? Anything you don't like? Remove it! Now go play!

Try overdyeing

Some of the most beautiful, rich-looking garments have only subtle variations in color. Accomplishing this when working with assorted balls of yarn can be remarkably simple and perhaps the most rewarding technique of all.

Imagine choosing contrast colors from your collection or from a yarn shop's sale bin, paying absolutely no attention to color (except that you would probably choose lighter rather than darker colors), only making sure that every-

A pile of yarn. . . .

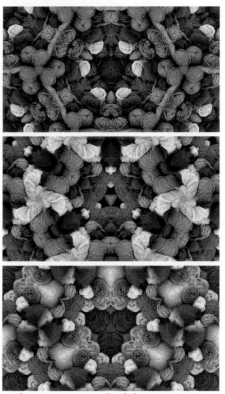

. . .becomes a wonderful repeating pattern. . .

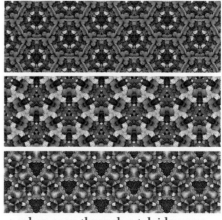

. . .when seen through a teleidoscope.

17

COLOR APPRECIATION
As we age, the color cones in our eyes mature and we are able to see—and appreciate—colors we could not when young. This explains why babies love bright, primary colors (red, blue, and yellow), young children love secondary colors (purple, green, and orange), and adults love more complex colors that are often described using more than one word (sharp yellow-green, dull blue-green, dusty pink).

Randy's Pullover *before* overdyeing

thing you choose is either 100% wool or 100% cotton. Then imagine knitting up a garment, paying absolutely no attention to what color you put where. What you will end up with may be a real "dog's breakfast," so be sure to take a photo of it. You will want a record of your "before" and "after," or no one will believe that one became the other! Then imagine giving the completed garment a dye bath in your favorite color, something darker than the colors you have used.

In the accompanying photos, you will see a range of swatches to which this has been done. Every swatch was knit exactly as the original. The results are quite amazing, don't you think?

I particularly liked the swatch that was dyed gray then a mix of olive green and tobacco brown. I think it's the most successful because dyeing it with three colors produced the most complex color. (As we age and the color cones in our eyes mature, we tend to prefer complex colors to simpler ones.)

One swatch was stripped of color and dyed a lighter color than the original. However the yarn became brittle and some of the wool fibers broke easily. I do not recommend this process.

Randy's Pullover (p. 90) is the result of this experimentation. I started with a rather unappealing green for the main color of the body, then used versions of this color for the edgings and sleeves. I used contrast colors that did not appeal to me in the least, which made a terrific and welcome dent in my yarn collection. For the overdyeing, I made a real soup: three parts gray, one part dark blue-green, one part tobacco brown, one part navy, and one part olive green. The result is subtle but wholly successful.

Randy's Pullover *after* overdyeing

For the dyeing process itself, you need to pay close attention to the directions on the package. Use the amount of dye suggested for the weight of the garment and for the amount of water you need to cover it. Use the required amount of mordant and a pot large enough that you can easily submerge and stir the garment. (I used a canning kettle.) Be sure the dye is completely dissolved before you add the garment to the water, and never add a dry garment to the dye solution.

If in doubt, ask lots of questions of the people who sell the dye. If their answers don't instill confidence, ask if the dye company has a number you can call before submitting your long hours of knitting to a process you are unsure of. If the first results of your dyeing are not successful, do not despair. You can dye it again, but in a darker color.

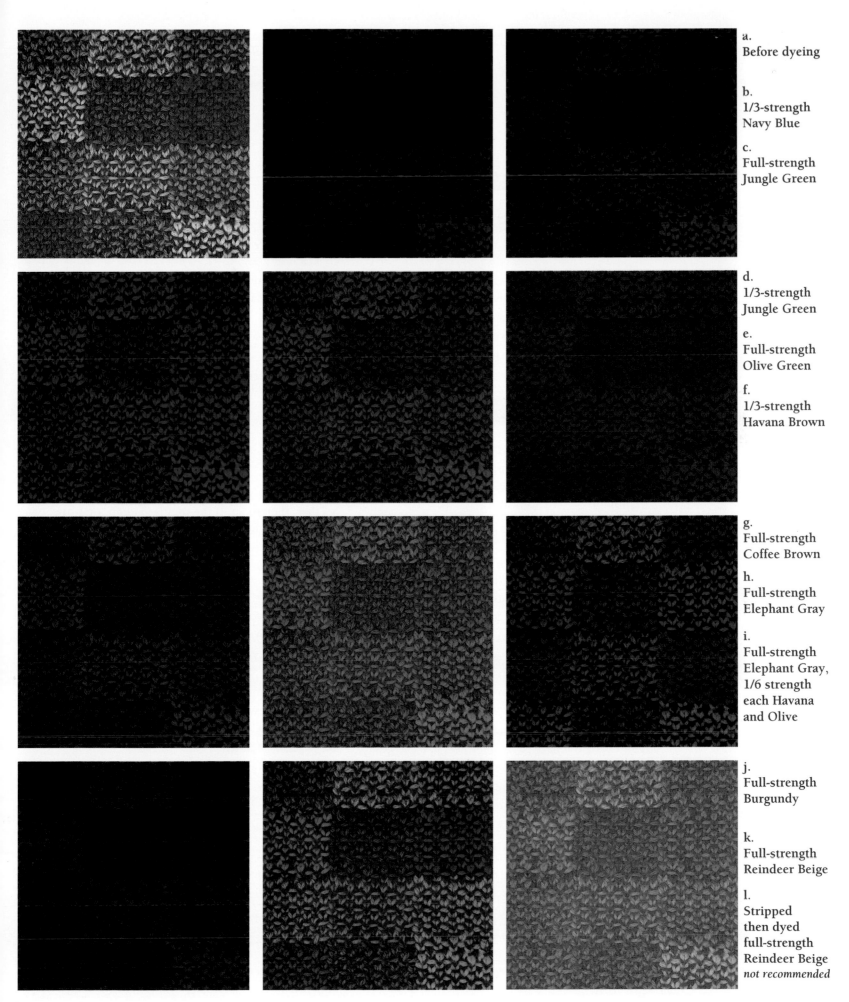

a.
Before dyeing

b.
1/3-strength
Navy Blue

c.
Full-strength
Jungle Green

d.
1/3-strength
Jungle Green

e.
Full-strength
Olive Green

f.
1/3-strength
Havana Brown

g.
Full-strength
Coffee Brown

h.
Full-strength
Elephant Gray

i.
Full-strength
Elephant Gray,
1/6 strength
each Havana
and Olive

j.
Full-strength
Burgundy

k.
Full-strength
Reindeer Beige

l.
Stripped
then dyed
full-strength
Reindeer Beige
not recommended

19

What yarns go together?

We aren't going to make much of a dent in your collection if you only combine yarns of the same weight and recommended needle gauge, yarns with the same texture, or yarns with the same care requirements.

Compatibility with respect to weight and gauge

The stitch and garment patterns in this book do not require yarns of precisely the same weight. For each garment pattern, you will be given a main color yarn weight and then a range of yarn weights for the contrast colors. The following chart explains the terminology used for these yarn weights:

Yarn Weight	Needle size	Sts to 4" (10cm)
Sport	4 (3.5mm)	23-24
DK	5-6 (3.75-4mm)	21-22
Worsted	7 (4.5mm)	19-20
Aran	8 (5mm)	17-18
Chunky	10 (6mm)	15-16

But sometimes, especially for novelty yarns or for those with no label, you just won't know what weight it is. Clearly, when you're using a variety of yarns in a garment, it's impractical to swatch each to determine the weight or gauge.

What to do? How do you work with this chart or with the following patterns if you don't know the weight of a particular yarn in your collection?

You can determine a yarn's weight by testing it against a yarn for which you have gauge information. Take the end of the mystery yarn and the end of the test yarn, and twist them once around each other so you are now holding one in the right hand and one in the left and each is doubled for a length of about 6". Now twist them in opposite directions.

What you have done is a) doubled the yarns, so if there is a difference between them you have intensified it, and b) twisted them to remove the "air" from them, so yarns which are tightly plied can be compared to yarns which are not. Now run your thumb and forefinger along the join between the yarns. If there is a bump at the join, the yarns are not the same weight. If the join does not produce a bump, then the yarns are compatible. (Thanks to Lee Andersen of Columbia, Maryland for this trick!)

If a yarn is too thick, perhaps you can thin it: remove one strand by grasping the strand you wish to remove and sliding the rest away. (You should only attempt this with relatively short lengths of yarn—no more than two yards.)

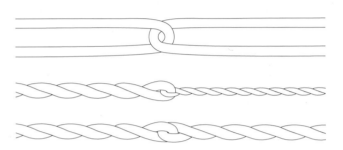

To test if yarns are the same weight, loop them together, then twist. If the join is smooth, they are similar in weight.

If the yarn is too thin, thicken it with a strand of sock or other thin yarn, either in the same color as the yarn itself or in the main color of the garment. If working in chunky weight yarns, you may use two strands of DK or worsted weight yarns combined.

Using these methods should help you determine what you have and a way to use it! Having said all this, however the stitch and garment patterns in this book are quite tolerant of different yarn weights.

To learn why, read the introductions to each stitch pattern section. That information will also help you understand the principles which will allow you to design your own "stash" styles.

Compatibility with respect to fiber and texture

Besides the obvious division by fiber content (and you may have yarn for which fiber content is an unknown quantity!), I think of yarns in three classes: 1) smooth and shiny, 2) fuzzy and bumpy, and 3) smooth and matte.

The smooth and shiny yarns include silk, mercerized cotton, viscose, ribbon, and other glitzy stuff. The fuzzy yarns are most commonly brushed mohairs, angoras, or brushed wools. The bumpy yarns are textured or novelty yarns with slubs, nubs, knots, or loops. The smooth and matte yarns are our plain wools, synthetics, unbrushed mohairs, linens, or unmercerized cottons.

These yarns are most demanding to the eye in the order in which they are presented in this list. The shiny yarns will grab the eye's attention first. The fuzzy or bumpy yarns will attract the eye's attention next. The smooth, matte yarns will be least demanding to the eye, thus providing a quieter visual alternative to the other yarns.

What does this mean when you are combining yarns? You may wish to forego the more demanding yarns, or you may try to be careful where you put them, or you may simply repeat them often enough that their focus is diffused. And you can use as much of the less demanding yarns as you wish.

Compatibility with respect to care and laundering

When combining yarns, you must consider whether they will respond in the same way to laundering or dry cleaning. Yarns that shrink against yarns that do not will distort the fabric. Yarns that bleed may diminish the beauty and intensity of the colors used.

The obvious solution would be to use yarns of the same fiber content and to launder them accordingly. But this isn't always a reasonable choice. Sometimes the label is unavailable, so you don't know the fiber content. Some yarns of the same fiber, particularly wool, launder differently, with some more susceptible to felting than others. And some colors in the same fiber will bleed while others will not.

What to do? First, check to see if any of your yarns will bleed. Practically speaking, you don't have to check

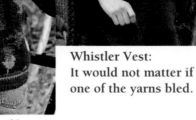

Whistler Vest:
It would not matter if one of the yarns bled.

Standing-in-a-pile-of-leaves
Pullover: It would matter if the dark color bled.

them all. Yarns most likely to bleed are cottons in dark or intense colors. If you suspect a yarn might bleed, dampen it and press it into a paper towel. If some color transfers, this yarn will bleed. Now you have to decide if this matters. If your garment is worked in a relatively limited color range with lots of this color, does it really matter if this yarn bleeds? Or if you are only using a couple of 2-yd lengths of this yarn in a garment filled with this color and others close to it, does that matter? No? Then go ahead and use it. But if you are planning to use this yarn as the main color for a garment with a variety of colors in contrast to it, it might really matter if this yarn bleeds. Save it for a single color garment.

After yarn choices are made and the garment is knit, launder the garment as you would for the most sensitive yarn used.

ABOUT WOOL
Its advantages are many: it "breathes" so is wearable in a range of temperatures, it retains heat so is warm when we need it to be; it is absorbent so is still comfortable when damp; and it has the greatest elasticity of any fiber so is the best choice for ribbings.

To best care for my wools, I wash them in a product called Eucalan; it has eucalyptus oil (to repel moths) and lanolin (to restore wool's natural oil). Wash as directed.

To avoid shrinkage, do not submit wool to either sudden change of temperature or to agitation when wet.

Avoid handling wool when wet since the fiber is significantly weakened.

YARN	NEEDLE	STITCHES	YARDAGE
WEIGHT	**SIZE**	**TO 4" (10CM)**	**APPROXIMATE**
Sport	4 (3.5mm)	23-24	165/50g
DK	5-6 (3.75-4mm)	21-22	140/50g
Worsted	7 (4.5mm)	19-20	115/50g
Aran	8 (5mm)	17-18	85/50g
Chunky	10 (6mm)	15-16	115/100g

THE YARNS

The patterns that follow describe yarns generically by weight and color. This table shows life-sized photos and descriptions for the five weights used. Colors are described by the twelve spokes of the color wheel: yellow, yellow-orange, orange, red-orange, red, red-purple, purple, blue-purple, blue, blue-green, green, and yellow-green.

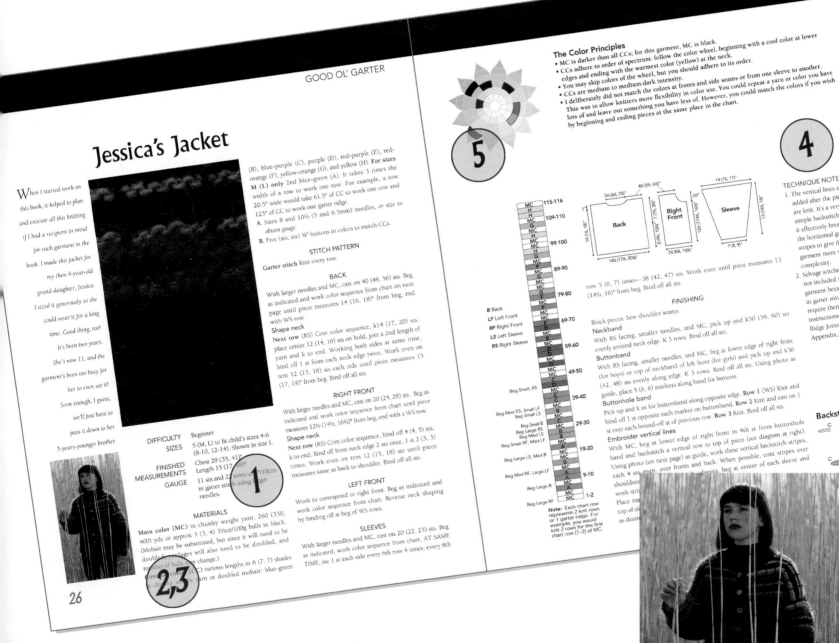

THE PRESENTATION

Each pattern is presented as a 2-page spread (or more), preceded or followed by a full-page photo. Closeup photos, the color wheel, and a brief discussion show the color principles at work.

1 GAUGE

Stitch gauge is important. Row gauge is less essential. For some patterns, you are instructed to work a number of complete stitch pattern repeats. In these cases, row gauge determines final length. You will decide which is more important: the finished measurement or a number of stitch pattern repeats.

2 MATERIALS

MC or CC

For more information on yarn weights, see What yarns go together? (p. 20).

MC Each pattern offers yarn amounts in terms of total yardage as well as approximate number of balls. These amounts are approximations only. It is not always easy to determine what's been used when working with partial balls of this and that! Always allow extra. Also, see How to know if you have enough? (p. 11) to determine if you have enough to work a row or area.

CC Each pattern says something like "2-yd lengths of various yarns." Full CC yardage amounts are given only where essential. Otherwise, simply use the required lengths of CC in as few as 7 colors…or as many as your heart desires!

Essentials We don't specify those important little items you always have at hand: markers, holders, scissors, tape measure, and a blunt needle.

3 MATERIALS

Buttons to match CC

For any or all cardigans, "buttons to match CC" could mean one CC or many! I frequently used un-matched buttons: they were fun, used up another of my "stashes," and echoed what was going on in the garment. Of course, you could also use MC buttons

4 NOTES

Any special techniques required in the instructions will be addressed in the Appendix, p. 138.

5 COLOR WHEEL

Whenever possible, the colors used in the garment are shown to full strength in the accompanying color wheel. Some colors (black, whites, grays, taupes, variegateds) cannot be shown on the color wheel. Also, the color wheel is a simplified tool, and you need not match colors exactly. For example, "medium intensity purple" would mean any bright purple you would put in your bin of purple yarn.

How to use these patterns

Choosing and developing stitch patterns that would make beautiful fabrics from lots of yarns and colors was my major task for this book. What follows are introductions to the stitch patterns I chose and garment patterns using each.

For you who are using this book as resource material only, after reading the introductions to the six stitch patterns I chose, I invite you to make use of this material and to continue an exploration of your own.

For you who wish to knit the patterns from this book, please read the points to the left. Note the differences between how these patterns and the ones you are accustomed to are written.

For you who are beginner knitters, there are three sweater patterns noted for beginners: Jessica's Jacket (p. 26), Ann's Purse (p. 106), and Riley's "Jeans" Pullover (p. 120). (Don't let the complicated chart for Riley's scare you. It's busy, yes, but that means that there's really no such thing as a mistake!)

Other garments could be simplified: Uncle Jeremy's Vest (p. 32), Topher's Pullovers (pp. 72 and 76), and The Whistler Vest (p. 78) could be worked in stripes rather than squares. Simply change contrast colors at the beginning of rows 3 and 4 (but not in mid-row), and repeat rows 1–4 for the pattern.

Although noted as intermediate, Caddy's Cardigan (pp. 48, 52) is a perfect first fairisle project because this color pattern repeat is so simple. And once you have mastered Knitting as Warp with Ann's Purse or Riley's Pullover, Tricia's Coat (p. 112) would not be a stretch at all.

For you who are intermediate knitters, there are three patterns noted as advanced because of the front point shaping. These could easily be converted to intermediate. Simply work each front with half the edging stitches of the back and proceed with the pattern from the place where the point shaping is completed.

SELVAGE STITCHES
For most of the garments in this book, selvage stitches are included. These will be taken into seam allowances when working Mattress stitch seams (see Appendix, p. 138). For garments in which selvage stitches were not included, the Technique Notes make this clear.

WORKING IN ENDS
Whenever possible, work in tails as you go: do not leave this task to the finishing of the garment. Weave beginning tails over the next row worked in the same direction. Weave end tails over the next row. See the Appendix, p. 138, for instructions on weaving.

PORTABLE KNITTING
Knitting with a variety of yarns and colors does not have to mean carrying half your yarn collection with the project. Cut lengths of CC as directed in each pattern (2yds? random lengths? 110"?), and carry these together with your MC.

COLOR WHEEL
If you do not like the colors shown in the photograph, take the pattern formed by those colors on the color wheel, rotate it until it covers colors you do like, and try working with the new selection. (See p. 141 for color wheels to use with this process.)

Good ol' Garter

Garter stitch is usually the first stitch pattern we learn because every row is knit. Then we move on to other, more complex stitch patterns and need to be reminded to come back and visit this lovely, simple old friend. In my work for this book I found garter stitch to be quite accommodating to different colors and yarns, so its options for exploration were a joy to discover!

The obvious place to begin working with garter stitch was with stripes. They offer a simple fabric and a beginner project—Jessica's Jacket. The vertical lines added after the garment is knit are an easy way to interrupt the horizontals and give the fabric added interest.

An option often overlooked is to use the wrong side of multi-colored garter stitch. Convince yourself by turning garter stitch stripes to the wrong side. There, the integration of color is really quite lovely. Following this, what would normally be the wrong side of colorfully striped garter was made the right side for Homer's Vest.

My experimentation with the wrong side of multi-colored garter stitch continued, and the result was an "outside carry" stitch pattern that I call Gander Blips. It's a terrific way to make maximum use of precious yarns—perhaps hand-dyed, hand-spun, or just expensive! If you try this stitch pattern, you will see that none of the contrast color is wasted on the inside of the garment.

Another feature of garter stitch that I explored was its ability to accommodate different yarns and colors. Uncle Jeremy's Vest uses garter stitch and a very simple intarsia pattern to integrate the main color with the contrasting yarns. The result is a subtly blended palette without the bulges and hollows that stockinette stitch would have produced in the same pattern.

The final and most intricate pattern in this section is the Inspired-by-the-Log-Cabin Jacket. It works with the ratio that garter stitch provides: 1 stitch = 2 rows. This ratio means that garter stitch allows multi-directional knitting quite easily—a highly creative avenue to explore!

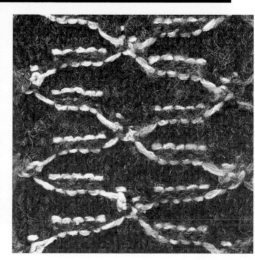

Two garments in this
section are worked in
intarsia. I do not use
or recommend bobbins.
For me, they tangle
terribly and add weight
to my work. It's also
a pain to wind them!
I much prefer to work
with lengths of yarn—
which I can pull free
to disentangle from
whatever mess I
have created.

Jessica's Jacket

When I started work on this book, it helped to plan and execute all this knitting if I had a recipient in mind for each garment in the book. I made this jacket for my then 9-year-old grand-daughter, Jessica. I sized it generously so she could wear it for a long time. Good thing, too! It's been two years. She's now 11, and the garment's been too busy for her to even see it! Soon enough, I guess, we'll just have to pass it down to her 5-years-younger brother.

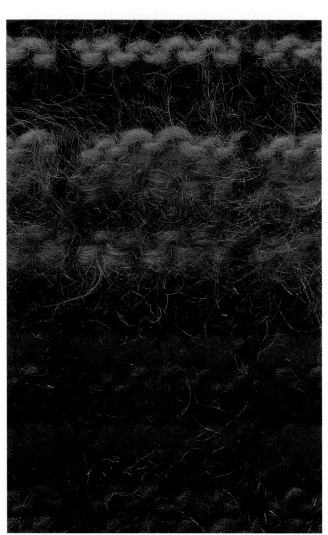

DIFFICULTY	Beginner
SIZES	S (M, L) to fit child's sizes 4-6 (8-10, 12-14). Shown in size L
FINISHED MEASUREMENTS	Chest 29 (35, 41)" Length 15 (17, 19)"
GAUGE	11 sts and 22 rows to 4"/10cm in garter stitch using larger needles.

MATERIALS

Main color (MC) in chunky weight yarn: 260 (330, 400) yds or approx 3 (3, 4) 3½oz/100g balls in black. (Mohair may be substituted, but since it will need to be doubled, yardages will also need to be doubled, and number of balls may change.)

Contrast colors (CC) various lengths in 6 (7, 7) shades in chunky weight yarn or doubled mohair: blue-green

(B), blue-purple (C), purple (D), red-purple (E), red-orange (F), yellow-orange (G), and yellow (H). **For sizes M (L) only** 2nd blue-green (A). It takes 3 times the width of a row to work one row. For example, a row 20.5" wide would take 61.5" of CC to work one row and 123" of CC to work one garter ridge.

A. Sizes 8 and 10½ (5 and 6.5mm) needles, *or size to obtain gauge.*

B. Five (six, six) ¾" buttons in colors to match CCs.

STITCH PATTERN

Garter stitch Knit every row.

BACK

With larger needles and MC, cast on 40 (48, 56) sts. Beg as indicated and work color sequence from chart on next page until piece measures 14 (16, 18)" from beg, end with WS row.

Shape neck

Next row (RS) Cont color sequence, k14 (17, 20) sts, place center 12 (14, 16) sts on hold, join a 2nd length of yarn and k to end. Working both sides at same time, bind off 1 st from each neck edge twice. Work even on rem 12 (15, 18) sts each side until piece measures 15 (17, 19)" from beg. Bind off all sts.

RIGHT FRONT

With larger needles and MC, cast on 20 (24, 28) sts. Beg as indicated and work color sequence from chart until piece measures 12½ (14½, 16½)" from beg, end with a WS row.

Shape neck

Next row (RS) Cont color sequence, bind off 4 (4, 5) sts, k to end. Bind off from neck edge 2 sts once, 1 st 2 (3, 3) times. Work even on rem 12 (15, 18) sts until piece measures same as back to shoulder. Bind off all sts.

LEFT FRONT

Work to correspond to right front. Beg as indicated and work color sequence from chart. Reverse neck shaping by binding off at beg of WS rows.

SLEEVES

With larger needles and MC, cast on 20 (22, 25) sts. Beg as indicated, work color sequence from chart, AT SAME TIME, inc 1 st each side every 6th row 4 times, every 8th

The Color Principles

- MC is darker than all CCs; for this garment, MC is black.
- CCs adhere to order of spectrum: follow the color wheel, beginning with a cool color at lower edges and ending with the warmest color (yellow) at the neck.
- You may skip colors of the wheel, but you should adhere to its order.
- CCs are medium to medium-dark intensity.
- I deliberately did not match the colors at fronts and side seams or from one sleeve to another. This was to allow knitters more flexibility in color use. You could repeat a yarn or color you have lots of and leave out something you have less of. However, you could match the colors if you wish by beginning and ending pieces at the same place in the chart.

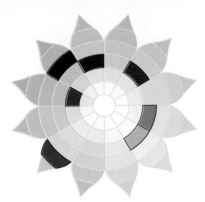

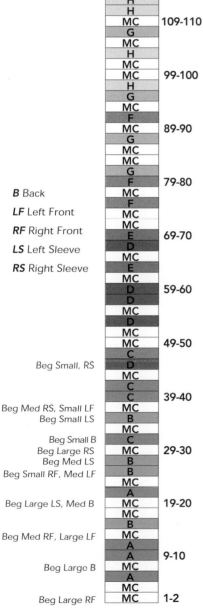

B Back
LF Left Front
RF Right Front
LS Left Sleeve
RS Right Sleeve

Beg Small, RS

Beg Med RS, Small LF
Beg Small LS

Beg Small B
Beg Large RS
Beg Med LS
Beg Small RF, Med LF

Beg Large LS, Med B

Beg Med RF, Large LF

Beg Large B

Beg Large RF

Note: Each chart row represents 2 knit rows or 1 garter ridge. For example, you would knit 2 rows for the first chart row (1–2) of MC.

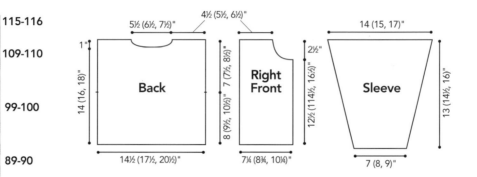

row 5 (6, 7) times—38 (42, 47) sts. Work even until piece measures 13 (14½, 16)" from beg. Bind off all sts.

FINISHING

Block pieces. Sew shoulder seams.

Neckband

With RS facing, smaller needles, and MC, pick up and k50 (56, 60) sts evenly around neck edge. K 3 rows. Bind off all sts.

Buttonband

With RS facing, smaller needles, and MC, beg at lower edge of right front (for boys) or top of neckband of left front (for girls) and pick up and k36 (42, 48) sts evenly along edge. K 3 rows. Bind off all sts. Using photo as guide, place 5 (6, 6) markers along band for buttons.

Buttonhole band

Pick up and k as for buttonband along opposite edge. **Row 1** (WS) Knit and bind off 1 st opposite each marker on buttonband. **Row 2** Knit and cast on 1 st over each bound-off st of previous row. **Row 3** Knit. Bind off all sts.

Embroider vertical lines

With MC, beg at lower edge of right front in 4th st from buttonhole band and backstitch a vertical row to top of piece (see diagram at right). Using photo (on next page) as guide, work these vertical backstitch stripes, each 4 sts apart, over fronts and back. When possible, cont stripes over shoulders and down back. On sleeves, beg at center of each sleeve and work stripes in every 4th stitch as for body.

Place markers 7 (7½, 8½)" down from shoulders on front and back. Sew top of sleeves between markers. Sew side and sleeve seams. Matching colors as desired, sew on buttons.

TECHNIQUE NOTES

1. The vertical lines are added after the pieces are knit. It's a very simple backstitch, but it effectively breaks up the horizontal garter stripes to give the garment more visual complexity.
2. Selvage stitches are not included in this garment because seams in garter stitch do not require them. (See instructions for Garter Ridge Joins in Appendix, p. 138)

Backstitch

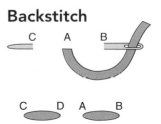

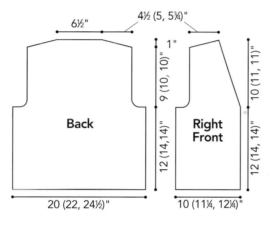

The Color Principles

- MCs are darker than CCs.
- MC1 (used in lower section) is darker than MC2 (used in upper section); CC1s (used in lower section) are darker than CC2s (used in upper section).
- CC1s are similar in color to MC2.
- CC1s are in same tonal range and CC2s are in same tonal range.
- An extremely limited color range is used (for this garment, charcoal, taupes, beiges, and off-whites). If working with more color, consider limiting yourself to two adjacent colors of the color wheel.

Back

6½"

12 (14, 14)"

20 (22, 24½)"

Right Front

4½ (5, 5¾)"

1"

9 (10, 10)"

10 (11, 11)"

12 (14, 14)"

10 (11¼, 12¼)"

TECHNIQUE NOTES

1. See Appendix, p. 138 for explanation of crochet cast-on method.
2. Use a separate length of CC for each 10-st square of the Garter st squares pattern. 2 rows of every 4 are worked in intarsia. When changing CCs, twist yarns to avoid holes.
3. Selvage stitches are not included in this garment because seams in garter stitch do not require them. (See Garter Ridge Joins in Appendix, p. 138.)

Shape armhole and neck

Next row (WS) Cont pat, bind off 6 (7, 8) sts—39 (43, 47) sts. **Next row** (RS) K1, k2tog (neck edge), cont pat to end. Shape armhole as for back, AT SAME TIME, dec 1 st at neck edge every 4th (6th, 6th) row 14 times more. Work even until armhole measures same as back to shoulder, end with a RS row. Shape shoulder as for back.

LEFT FRONT

Work as for right front, reversing all shaping. **For sizes S, L only** End each row by working last 5 sts with 1½ yd in CC1 or CC2. **For all sizes** Work pocket lining as foll: Place pocket at change between MC1 and MC2 to match right front by k10 sts at beg of RS row, k next 20 sts, turn, p20; turn and work 48 rows rows more in St st, complete pocket to match right front.

FINISHING

Block pieces. Sew shoulder seams. Work all bands with MC1 or MC2 as desired.

Armhole bands

With RS facing, smaller needles, and MC, beg at armhole edge and pick up and k1 st for each bound-off st, and 1 st for each garter ridge around armhole. K 1 row. Bind off all sts.

Buttonband

Note For women, beg at center back and k15 sts from holder, then pick up along left front. For men, beg at lower right front edge, pick up sts along right front, then k15 sts from holder.

With RS facing, smaller needles, and MC, beg as noted above and pick up sts as foll: 1 st for each garter ridge to beg of V-neck shaping, work k1, yo, k1 in st at point of V, 1 st for each garter ridge to end. After picking up sts, k 1 row, then bind off all sts. Sew buttons between band and garment using large photo on p. 34 as guide to button placement and button color.

Buttonhole band

Place markers on right or left front opposite buttons on buttonband. Pick up and k sts as for buttonband (including rem sts at back neck), AT SAME TIME, cast on 2 sts at each marker (instead of picking up 2 sts) for buttonhole. K 1 row, then bind off all sts.

Sew bands at back neck. Sew side seams, including armbands. Sew sides of pocket linings, then tack corners to WS.

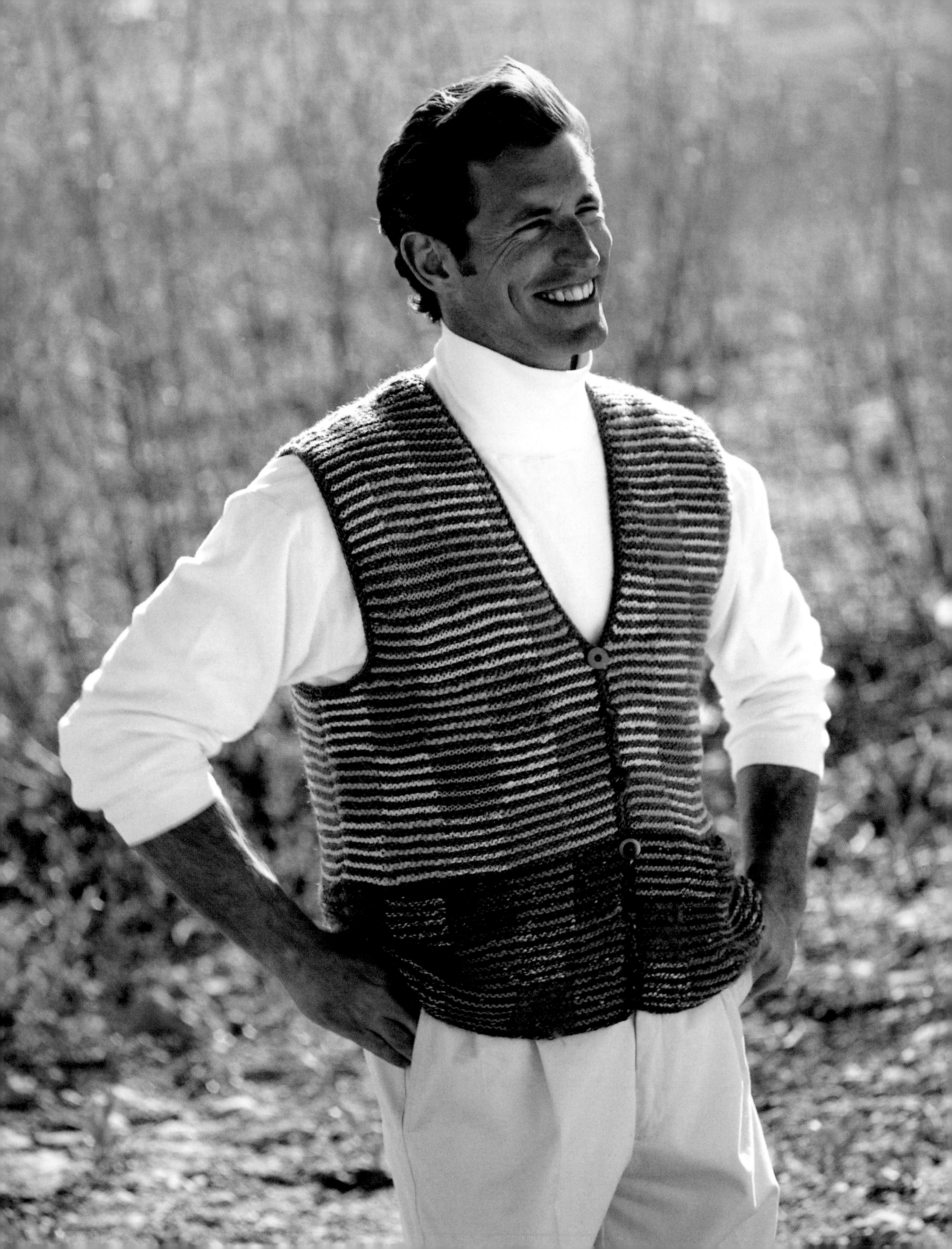

Gander Blips Vest

I was traveling around Newfoundland one summer. Cod fishing had been halted, so the towns were fairly quiet. I spent much of my evenings figuring out how to carry yarns on the outside of the knit fabric, using a kind of garter stitch, to make maximum use of minimum lengths of yarn. It was in Gander that I finished charting the stitch pattern.

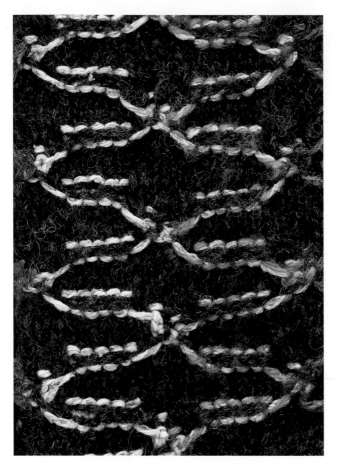

STITCH PATTERNS

Double moss st trim (multiple of 4).
Row 1 (RS) *K2 MC, p2 CC; rep from*. **Row 2** *K2 MC, p2 CC; rep from*. **Row 3** Change CC: *P2 CC, k2 MC; rep from*. **Row 4** *P2 CC, k2 MC; rep from*. Rep rows 1–4 for trim pat, changing CC every 2 rows.
Gander blips (multiple of 18 sts).
Note Change CC colors as indicated on chart.
Row 1 (RS) With MC, p5, k4, with CC, p5, with MC, k4.
Row 2 With MC, p1, with CC, k1, with MC, p2, k5, p9.
Row 3 With MC, k15, with CC, p1, with another CC, p1, with MC, k1. **Row 4** With MC, p1, k1, with CC, k1, with MC, p15. **Row 5** With CC, p5, with MC, k10, p1, k2.
Row 6 With MC, p4, with CC, k5, with MC, p4, k5.
Row 7 With MC, k6, with CC, p1, with MC, k2, p5, k4.
Row 8 With MC, p10, with CC, k1, with next CC, k1, with MC, p6. **Row 9** With MC, k6, p1, with CC, p1, with MC, k10. **Row 10** With MC, p10, k1, p2, with CC, k5. Rep these 10 rows for Gander blips pat.

BACK

With smaller needles and MC, cast on 98 (106, 114) sts. Working first and last st in St st as selvage, work 10 rows in trim pat. Change to larger needles. With MC, k 1 row and inc 6 (6, 8) sts evenly across—104 (112, 122) sts. P 1 row. **Beg chart: Row 1** (RS) K1 (selvage), beg as indicated and work to rep line, work 18-st rep 5 (5, 6) times, end as indicated, k1 (selvage). Cont chart pat as established until piece measures 10 (11, 12)" from beg, end with a WS row.
Shape armhole
Cont pat, bind off 5 sts at beg of next 2 rows—94 (102, 112) sts. Dec 1 st each side every other row 8 (8, 9) times—78 (86, 94) sts. Work even until armhole is 9 (9½, 10)", end with a WS row. Mark center 30 (32, 36) sts.
Shape back neck and shoulder
Bind off 5 (6, 6) sts beg next 2 rows. **Next row** Bind off 5 (6, 6) sts (shoulder edge), work to marked sts, turn. Bind off 1 st (neck edge), work across, turn. Bind off 5 (6, 7) sts, work across, turn. Bind off 1 st, work across, turn. Bind off rem sts. Place marked sts on hold. With RS facing, join yarn and cont pat across left shoulder. Shape as for right shoulder as foll: At shoulder edge, bind off 5 (6, 6) sts once, 5 (6, 7) sts once, then bind off rem sts, AT SAME TIME, bind off 1 st at neck edge twice.

DIFFICULTY	Intermediate
SIZES	S (M, L). Shown in size M.
FINISHED MEASUREMENTS	Bust 41½ (45, 49)" Length 20 (21½, 23)"
GAUGE	20 sts and 26 rows to 4"/10cm in Gander blips pat using larger needles.

MATERIALS

Main color (MC) in worsted weight yarn: 500 (600, 700) yds or approx 5 (6, 7) 1¾oz/50g balls in charcoal gray.
Contrast colors (CC) in various weights (DK to chunky, textured or fuzzy): maximum 5 yd lengths of lighter grays for Gander blips pat and various lengths of CC for trim pat; total CC approx 160 (170, 180) yds. (It takes twice the width of a row to work one trim pat row. For example, it takes 40" of CC to work a row that is 20" wide.)
A. Sizes 5 and 7 (3.75 and 4.5mm) needles, *or size to obtain gauge.*
B. Size 5 (3.75mm) circular needle, 24" (60cm).
C. Six ½" buttons to match CCs.

The Color Principles
• MC is darker than CCs.
• For this garment, only one color is used: gray (light to medium intensity for CCs and dark intensity for MC).

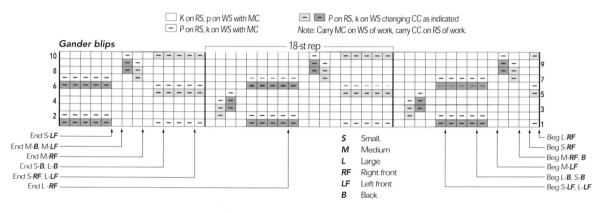

Legend:
☐ K on RS, p on WS with MC
⊟ P on RS, k on WS with MC

⊟ ■ P on RS, k on WS changing CC as indicated
Note: Carry MC on WS of work, carry CC on RS of work.

Gander blips
18-st rep

End S-LF
End M-B, M-LF
End M-RF
End S-B, L-B
End S-RF, L-LF
End L -RF

S   Small,
M   Medium
L   Large
RF   Right front
LF   Left front
B   Back

Beg L-RF
Beg S-RF
Beg M-RF, B
Beg M-LF
Beg L-B, S-B
Beg S-LF, L-LF

RIGHT FRONT

With smaller needles and MC, cast on 50 (54, 58) sts. Working first and last st in St st as selvage, work 10 rows in trim pat. Change to larger needles and MC. K 1 row and inc 2 (2, 4) sts—52 (56, 62) sts. **Beg chart: Row 1** (RS) K1 (selvage), beg as indicated and work to rep line, work 18-st rep twice, end as indicated, k1 (selvage). Cont chart pat as established until piece measures same as back to armhole, end with a RS row.

Shape armhole

Next row (WS) Cont pat, bind off 5 sts, work to end—47 (51, 57) sts. Dec 1 st at armhole edge every other row 8 (8, 9) times—39 (43, 48) sts. Work even until armhole measures 7 (7½, 8)", end with a WS row.

Shape neck and shoulder

Next row (RS) Bind off 10 (11, 12) sts, work to end—29 (32, 36) sts. Bind off at neck edge 3 sts once and **for size L only**, 3 sts once more. **For all sizes** Bind off 1 st at neck edge 4 (4, 3) times, then work even, AT SAME TIME, when armhole measures same as back to shoulder, bind off 5 (6, 6) sts twice, 5 (6, 7) sts once. Bind off rem sts.

LEFT FRONT

Work to correspond to Right Front, reversing all shaping.

FINISHING

Block pieces. Sew shoulder seams.

Neck trim

With RS facing, circular needle, and MC, pick up and k98 (102, 106) sts around neck edge, including sts on hold. Cut yarn and return to beg of row, ready to work RS row. Work 6 rows in trim pat. With MC, bind off all sts knitwise.

Buttonband

With RS facing, circular needle, and MC, beg at left neck edge and pick up and k82 (90, 98) sts (approx 3 sts for every 4 rows) along left front. Cut yarn. Return to beg of row, ready to work a RS row. Work 6 rows in trim pat. **Next row** (RS) With MC, k and dec 6 (8, 10) sts evenly across—76 (82, 88) sts. K 1 row, then p 1 row. Bind off all sts knitwise. Sew 6 buttons evenly spaced on button band.

Buttonhole band

With RS facing, circular needle, and MC, beg at lower right front edge and pick up and k82 (90, 98) sts to neck as for buttonband. Cut yarn. Return to beg of row, ready to work a RS row. Work as for buttonband, working 6 eyelet buttonholes opposite buttons on buttonband on row 3 of trim pat as foll: work 2 tog, yo. On next row, work yo's into trim pat.

Armbands

With RS facing, smaller needles, and MC, beg at armhole edge and pick up and k1 st for each bound-off st and 3 sts for every 4 rows around armhole. K 1 row, then p 1 row. Bind off all sts knitwise.

Sew side seams, including armbands.

TECHNIQUE NOTES

1. The written version of Gander blips pat gives the 18-st pattern repeat. Refer to chart for stitch pat at beg and end of rows.

2. In Gander blips pat, CCs are carried vertically on RS of work; MC is carried on WS of work.

3. You may use a single, hand-dyed or specialty yarn as CC. However, you will still need to cut this yarn to the length specified and carry each piece, individually, up the right side of the fabric.

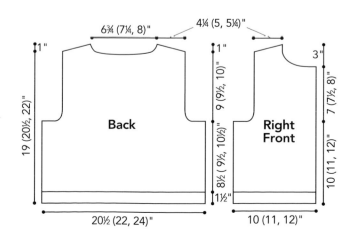

6¾ (7¼, 8)"   4¼ (5, 5¼)"
1"   1"   3"
19 (20½, 22)"   9 (9½, 10)"   7 (7½, 8)"
8½ (9½, 10½)"
Back   **Right Front**
10 (11, 12)"
1½"
20½ (22, 24)"   10 (11, 12)"

Gander Blips Jacket

I made this jacket before the vest, and I originally made it as a vest. But its brighter color range seemed to make it more appropriate as a jacket, so I removed the armhole edging and added sleeves. It might be cool to make sleeves but also have yarn for the armhole edging so you could have a vest for the warmer months and a jacket for the cooler—if you are willing to do all the switching back and forth! To make this Aran weight garment a vest, just follow the armhole band notes in the previous pattern.

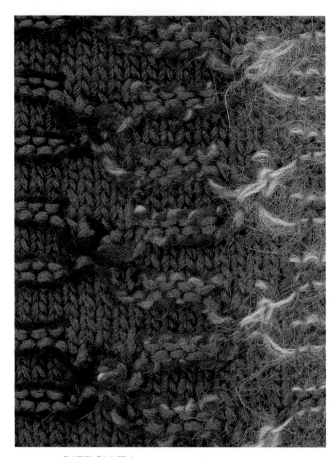

DIFFICULTY	Intermediate
SIZES	S (M, L). Shown in size M.
FINISHED MEASUREMENTS	Bust 45½ (49½, 53½)" Length 20 (21½, 23)"
GAUGE	18 sts and 26 rows to 4"/10cm in Gander blips pat using larger needles.

MATERIALS

Main color (MC) in Aran weight yarn: 900 (1000, 1100) yds or approx 11 (12, 13) 1¾oz/50g balls in dark blue-green.

Contrast colors (CC) in various weights (worsted to chunky, textured or fuzzy): maximum 5 yd lengths of light-medium to dark intensity reds, red-purples, purples, blue-purples, and blue-greens for Gander blips pat and various lengths of CC for trim pat; total CC approx 190 (200, 210) yds. (It takes twice the width of a row to work one trim pat row. For example, it takes 40" of CC to work a row that is 20" wide.)

A. Sizes 6 and 8 (4 and 5mm) needles, *or size to obtain gauge.*

B. Size 6 (4mm) circular needle, 24" (60cm).

C. Six ½" buttons in CCs.

STITCH PATTERNS

Double moss st trim (multiple of 4)
Row 1 (RS) *K2 MC, p2 CC; rep from*. **Row 2** *K2 MC, p2 CC; rep from*. **Row 3** Change CC: *P2 CC, k2 MC; rep from*. **Row 4** *P2 CC, k2 MC; rep from*. Rep rows 1–4 for trim pat, changing CC every 2 rows.
Gander blips (multiple of 18 sts)
See written pat for 18-st rep on p. 36.

BACK

With smaller needles and MC, cast on 98 (106, 114) sts. Working first and last st in St st as selvage, work 10 rows in trim pat. Change to larger needles. With MC, k 1 row and inc 6 (6, 8) sts evenly across—104 (112, 122) sts. P 1 row. **Beg chart: Row 1** (RS) K1 (selvage), beg as indicated and work to rep line, work 18-st rep 5 (5, 6) times, end as indicated, k1 (selvage). Cont chart pat as established until piece measures 10 (11, 12)" from beg, end with a WS row.
Shape armhole
Cont pat, bind off 5 sts at beg of next 2 rows—94 (102, 112) sts. Dec 1 st each side every other row 8 (8, 9) times—78 (86, 94) sts. Work even until armhole measures 9 (9½, 10)", end with a WS row. Mark center 30 (32, 36) sts.
Shape back neck and shoulder
Bind off 5 (6, 6) sts beg next 2 rows. **Next row** Bind off 5 (6, 6) sts (shoulder edge), work to marked sts, turn. Bind off 1 st (neck edge), work across, turn. Bind off 5 (6, 7) sts, work across, turn. Bind off 1 st, work across, turn. Bind off rem sts. Place marked sts on hold. With RS facing, join yarn and cont pat across left shoulder. Shape as for right shoulder as foll: At shoulder edge, bind off 5 (6, 6) sts twice, 5 (6, 7) sts once, then bind off rem sts, AT SAME TIME, bind off 1 st at neck edge twice.

RIGHT FRONT

With smaller needles and MC, cast on 50 (54, 58) sts. Working first and last st in St st as selvage, work 10 rows in trim pat. Change to larger needles and MC. K 1 row and inc 2 (2, 4) sts—52 (56, 62) sts. **Beg chart: Row 1** (RS) K1 (selvage), beg as indicated and work to rep line, work 18-st rep twice, end as indicated, k1 (selvage). Cont chart pat as established until piece measures same as back to armhole, end with a RS row.

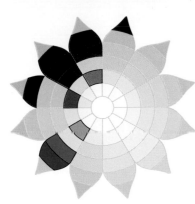

The Color Principles
- MC (for this garment, dark intensity blue-green) is darker than most CCs.
- CCs are light-medium to dark intensity, covering one–half of the color wheel—for this garment, the cool side, from red to blue-green.

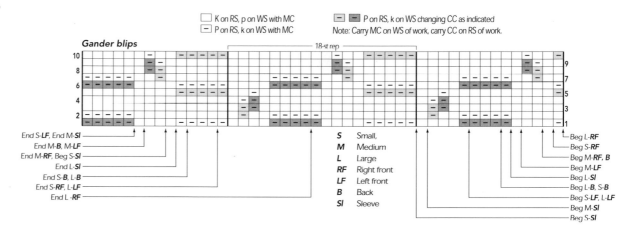

☐ K on RS, p on WS with MC
⊟ P on RS, k on WS with MC

⊟ ▬ P on RS, k on WS changing CC as indicated
Note: Carry MC on WS of work, carry CC on RS of work.

Gander blips

18-st rep

End S-**LF**, End M-**Sl**
End M-**B**, M-**LF**
End M-**RF**, Beg S-**Sl**
End L-**Sl**
End S-**B**, L-**B**
End S-**RF**, L-**LF**
End L -**RF**

S Small,
M Medium
L Large
RF Right front
LF Left front
B Back
Sl Sleeve

Beg L-**RF**
Beg S-**RF**
Beg M-**RF**, **B**
Beg M-**LF**
Beg L-**Sl**
Beg L-**B**, S-**B**
Beg S-**LF**, L-**LF**
Beg M-**Sl**
Beg S-**Sl**

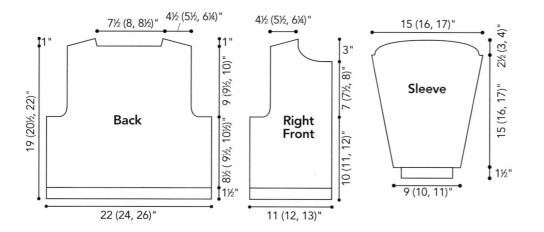

Back — 19 (20½, 22)" ; 22 (24, 26)" ; 7½ (8, 8½)" ; 4½ (5½, 6¼)" ; 1" ; 8½ (9½, 10½)" ; 1½"

Right Front — 4½ (5½, 6¼)" ; 1" ; 3" ; 9 (9½, 10)" ; 7 (7½, 8)" ; 10 (11, 12)" ; 11 (12, 13)"

Sleeve — 15 (16, 17)" ; 2½ (3, 4)" ; 15 (16, 17)" ; 1½" ; 9 (10, 11)"

TECHNIQUE NOTES
1. In Gander blips pat, CCs are carried vertically on RS of work; MC is carried on WS of work
2. You may use a single, hand-dyed or specialty yarn as CC. However, you will still need to cut this yarn to the lengths specified and carry each piece, individually, up the right side of the fabric.

Shape armhole
Next row (WS) Cont pat, bind off 5 sts, work to end—47 (51, 57) sts. Dec 1 st at armhole edge every other row 8 (8, 9) times—39 (43, 48) sts. Work even until armhole measures 7 (7½, 8)", end with a WS row.

Shape neck and shoulder
Next row (RS) Bind off 10 (11, 12) sts, work to end—29 (32, 36) sts. Bind off at neck edge 3 sts once and **for size L only,** 3 sts once more. **For all sizes** Bind off 1 st at neck edge 4 (4, 3) times, then work even, AT SAME TIME, when armhole measures same as back to shoulder, bind off 5 (6, 6) sts twice, 5 (6, 7) sts once. Bind off rem sts.

LEFT FRONT
Work to correspond to right front, reversing all shaping.

SLEEVES
With smaller needles and MC, cast on 38 (40, 46) sts.

Working first and last st in St st as selvage, work 10 rows in trim pat. Change to larger needles. With MC, k and inc 6 sts evenly across—44 (48, 52) sts. P 1 row. Cont selvage sts, beg and end as indicated and work Gander blips pat, AT SAME TIME, inc 1 st each side (working incs into pat) every 6th row 12 (12, 13) times—68 (72, 78) sts. Work even until piece measures 16½ (17½, 18½)" from beg, end with a WS row.

Shape cap
Cont pat, bind off 5 sts at beg of next 2 rows—58 (62, 68) sts. Dec 1 st each side every other row 4 (6, 9) times—50 sts. Bind off 2 sts at beg of 4 rows, 3 sts at beg of 2 rows, 5 sts at beg of next 2 rows. Bind off rem 26 sts.

FINISHING
Block pieces. Sew shoulder seams. Work neck and front bands as for vest, p. 37. Set in sleeves. Sew side and sleeve seams. Sew on buttons.

Inspired-by-the-Log-Cabin Jacket

The squares of this garment are loosely based upon the Log Cabin quilt block. The squares are offset against each other by working with a wonderful feature of garter stitch— the gauge ratio of one stitch to two rows. This ratio means that multi-directional knitting is simplified. You could use this information, and even the structure of this pattern, to make a garment simpler than this one by just not doing the intarsia work within the squares—in other words using only one CC for each square.

DIFFICULTY	Advanced
SIZES	S (M, L). Shown in size M.
FINISHED MEASUREMENTS	Bust 40 (44, 48)" Length 24"
GAUGE	16 sts and 32 rows to 4"/10cm in garter st using larger needles.

MATERIALS

Main colors (MC) in worsted weight yarn: 1600 (1700, 1800) yds, approx 14 (15, 16) 1¾oz/50g balls in medium intensity gray (MC).

Contrast colors (CC) in DK to Aran weight yarn of light to medium intensity: 48" lengths of off-whites (CC1); 36" lengths of red-oranges or oranges (CC2); 42" lengths of yellows (CC3), 51" lengths of yellow-greens (CC4), 57" lengths of greens or blue-greens (CC5), approx 100 yds (or one 50g ball) extra of CC5 for sleeves and trims.

A. Sizes 5 and 7 (3.75 and 4.5mm) needles, *or size to obtain gauge.*

B. Six ⅞" buttons to match any CCs.

Notes 1 Jacket is worked in strips of garter squares. Each square is connected to the previous square as it is knit. The strips are then sewn together to form the jacket. **2** Use larger needles to work all strips.

STRIP I (Lower edge of back to lower edge of front)
Work Full Square A: With MC, cast on 17 sts. Working in garter st (k every row), work rows 1–34 of Full Square A chart. Turn and cast on 17 sts at end of row 34.
Work Full Square B and join to Square A: (row 1 is a RS row) **Row 1** (RS) K16 MC, sl next st, k 1 from Square A, then psso. **Row 2** K17 MC. **Row 3** K16 CC5, sl next st, k1 from Square A, then psso. **Row 4** K17 CC5. In same way, work color pat from chart rows 5–34 and join the 2 squares every RS row.
Cut yarn. As desired, either place 17 sts from row 34 on hold (to graft them to other strips when assembling jacket) or bind them off (to sew them to other strips when assembling jacket). Hold the two squares with RS facing you, Row 1 of Square A at bottom and sts on hold (or bound-off) at left. Thread needle through 17 garter loops along top of Square B, ready to work a RS row. Cont to work Squares A and B until a total of 12 squares have been worked. Mark first Square A as lower edge of back. Mark final Square B as lower edge of left front.

STRIP II (Lower edge of front to lower edge of back)
Work as for Strip I. Mark first Square A as lower edge of right front. Mark final Square B as lower edge of back.

STRIP III (Right center back)
Beg with Full Square A chart and work as for Strip I until 5 squares are complete, casting on 12 sts at end of last square. Work 6th square from Partial Square chart over 12 sts and 34 rows as foll: **Row 1** (RS) K11 MC, sl next st, k1 from Square A, psso. **Row 2** K12 MC. **Row 3** K11 CC5, sl next st, k1 from Square A, psso. **Row 4** K12 CC5. **Rows 5–10** Rep rows 1–4, then 1–2. **Row 11** K7 CC1, with CC4, k4, sl next st, k1 from Square A, psso. **Row 12** K5 CC4, k7 CC1. **Rows 13–24** Rep rows 9–12 a total of 3 times. **Rows 25–26** Rep rows 1–2. **Row 27** K7 CC3, with CC4, k4, sl next st, k1 from Square A, psso. **Row 28** K5 CC4, k7 CC3. **Rows 29–32** Rep rows 25–28. **Rows 33–34** Rep rows 1–2. Place 12 sts on hold. First square is lower edge of back; final square is back neck edge.

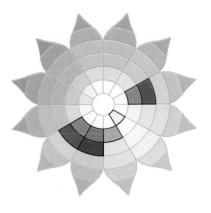

The Color Principles

- MC—for this garment, medium-intensity gray—is darker than CCs.
- For this garment CCs are light to medium intensity, CC1 is off-white; CC2 is red-orange or orange; CC3 is yellow; CC4 is yellow-green; CC5 is green or blue-green.
- CC2–5 follow the order of the color wheel, beginning with warm colors and ending with cool colors. Colors on the wheel may be skipped, but its order should be adhered to.
- For this garment, extra CC5s are used for the underarms and trims.
- Other colors of the wheel may be used, but CC for underarms should be the coolest color used.

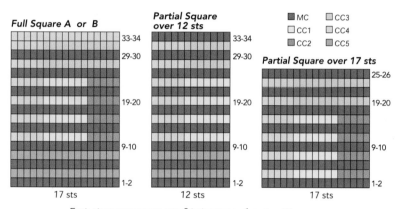

Full Square A or B
33-34
29-30
19-20
9-10
1-2
17 sts

Partial Square over 12 sts
33-34
29-30
19-20
9-10
1-2
12 sts

Partial Square over 17 sts
25-26
19-20
9-10
1-2
17 sts

■ MC	□ CC3
□ CC1	□ CC4
■ CC2	■ CC5

Each chart row represents 2 knit rows or 1 garter ridge.

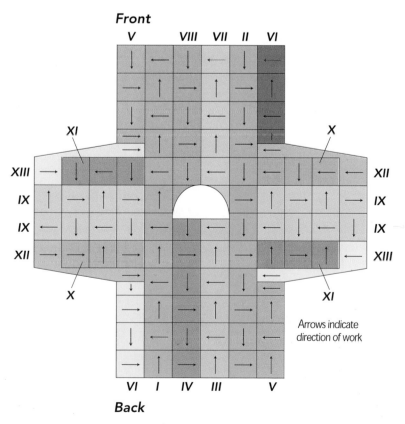

Front

V   VIII VII II VI

XI   X

XIII   XII

IX   IX

IX   IX

XII   XIII

X   XI

VI   I   IV   III V

Back

Arrows indicate direction of work

STRIP IV Left center back

With MC, cast on 17 sts. Work 26 rows of Partial Square over 17 sts. Beg with Full Square B, work 5 complete squares as for Strip I. Place 17 sts of final Square B on hold. First square is back neck edge; final square is lower edge of back.

STRIP V Underarm

For all sizes Make 2, one for right back, the other for left front.

Size S only With MC, cast on 7 sts. **First square: Rows 1–2** K with MC. **Rows 3–4** K with CC5. **Rows 5–32** [K 2 rows MC, k 2 rows CC4] 7 times. **Rows 33–34** K with MC. Turn and cast on 17 sts at end of row 34.

2nd square: Row 1 K16 MC, sl next st, k1 from first square, psso. **Row 2** K17 MC. **Row 3** K12 CC3, k4 CC4, sl next st, k1 from first square, psso. **Row 4** K5 CC4, k12 CC3. **Rows 5–12** Rep rows 1–4. **Rows 13–14** Rep rows 1–2. Place 17 sts on hold.

3rd square With RS facing and original cast-on edge at bottom, slip needle through 17 garter loops at top of piece ready to work a RS row. Rep rows 1–34 of first square, casting on 5 sts at end of row 34.

4th square Rep rows 1–4 of 2nd square 3 times. Then rep rows 1–2 of 2nd square once. Place 5 sts on hold.

Size M only

With MC, cast on 13 sts. **First square** Work 34 rows of Partial Square chart over 12 sts with foll change: **On RS rows**, k first st with MC, then work 12 sts in pat. **On WS rows**, work 12 sts in pat, then k last st with MC. Cast on 17 sts at end of row 34.

2nd square Work Partial Square chart over

TECHNIQUE NOTES

1. 2 rows out of every 4 are worked in intarsia. Twist yarns at CC change to avoid holes.

2. Begin each strip with one square. Other squares are worked one at a time and joined to each other by knitting "live" stitches tog or by knitting from loops along side edge.

3. For ease in working, mark RS of first square in each strip. Keep careful track of rows.

4. When joining strips, graft open or bound-off sts of one square to side edge of second square. (See Grafting in Appendix, p. 138.)

5. Mark each strip as you finish for ease in assembling, or sew strips tog as you go.

17 sts. Place 17 sts on hold or bind off.

3rd square With RS facing and original cast-on edge at bottom, slip needle through 13 garter loops at top of piece, ready to work a RS row. Rep first square, casting on 5 sts at end of row 34.

4th square: Row 1 K4 MC, sl next st, k1 from 3rd square, psso. **Row 2** K5 MC. **Row 3** K4 CC5, sl next st, k1 from 3rd square, psso. **Row 4** K5 CC5. **Rows 5–24** Rep rows 1–4. **Rows 25–26** Rep rows 1–2. Place 5 sts on hold or bind off.

Size L only

With MC, cast on 17 sts. **First, 2nd and 3rd squares** Work Full Square A, then B, then A, casting on 5 sts at end of last row of 3rd square. **4th square: Row 1** K4 MC, sl next st, k1 from 3rd square, psso. **Row 2** K5 MC. **Row 3** K4 CC5, sl next st, k1 from 3rd square, psso. **Row 4** K5 CC5. **Rows 5–32** Rep rows 1–4. **Rows 33–34** Rep rows 1–2. Place 5 sts on hold or bind off.

STRIP VI Underarm

For all sizes Make 2, one for right front, the other for left back.

Size S only

With MC, cast on 7 sts. **First square: Rows 1–8** [K 2 rows MC, k 2 rows CC5] twice. **Rows 9–10** K with MC, casting on 17 sts at end of row 10.

2nd square Work 14 rows of 2nd square of Strip V, size S. Place 17 sts on hold or bind off.

3rd square With RS facing and original cast-on edge at bottom, sl needle through 7 garter loops at top of piece, ready to work a RS row. **Rows 1–8** [K 2 rows MC, k 2 rows CC5] twice. **Rows 9–32** [K 2 rows MC, k 2 rows CC4] 6 times. **Rows 33–34** K with MC, casting on 17 sts at end of row 34.

4th square Rep 14 rows of 2nd square.

Size M only

With MC, cast on 13 sts. **First square: Rows 1–8** [K 2 rows MC, k 2 rows CC5] twice. **Rows 9–10** K with MC, casting on 17 sts at end of row 10.

2nd square Work Partial Square chart over 17 sts. Place 17 sts on hold or bind off.

3rd square With RS facing and original cast-on edge at bottom, sl needle through 13 garter loops at top of piece, ready to work a RS row. Work 34 rows of Partial Square

chart over 12 sts. On RS rows, k first st with MC, then work 12 sts in pat. On WS rows, work 12 sts in pat, then k last st with MC. Cast on 17 sts at end of row 34.

4th square Work Partial square chart over 17 sts. Place 17 sts on hold or bind off.

Size L only

With MC, cast on 17 sts. **First square: Rows 1–8** [K 2 rows MC, k 2 rows CC5] twice. **Rows 9–10** K with MC, casting on 17 sts at end of row 10. Work Full Square B, then A, then B.

STRIP VII Right center front

With MC, cast on 17 sts. Work Full Square A and place 17 sts of row 34 on hold or bind off. With RS facing and cast-on edge at bottom, sl needle through 17 garter loops along right side of square, ready to work a RS row. Work Full Square A again, then alternate B and A until there are 5 full squares in strip.

Shape neck Hold strip with RS facing and first square at top. Working from left to right, sl needle through first 9 garter loops. **Rows 1–2** K with MC. **Rows 3–4** With CC5, bind off 3sts, k across; turn, k6. **Rows 5–6** With MC, bind off 2 sts, k across; turn, k 4. **Rows 7–8** With CC5, bind off 1 st, k across; turn, k3. **Rows 9–10** With MC, bind off 1 st, k across; turn, k2. **Row 11** With MC, bind off 1 st. Fasten off.

STRIP VIII Left center front

With MC, cast on 17 sts. Beg with Full Square A, work 5 full squares. Do not cast on 17 sts at end of 5th square. **Shape neck. Rows 1–2** K9 MC; turn, bind off 3 sts, k across. **Rows 3–4** K6 CC5; turn, bind off 2 sts, k across. **Rows 5–6** K4 MC; turn, bind off 1 st, k across. **Rows 7–8** K3 CC5; turn, bind off 1 st, k across. **Rows 9–10** K2 MC; turn, bind off 1 st. Fasten off.

STRIP IX Top of sleeves

Make 4. With MC, cast on 17 sts. Work Full Square A and place 17 sts of row 34 on hold or bind off. With RS facing and cast-on edge at bottom, sl needle through 17 garter loops along right side of square, ready to work a RS row. Work Square A, then B, then A.

STRIP X Side edge of sleeves

Make 2. With MC, cast on 17 sts. Work Full Square A, then B, then A.

STRIP XI Side edge of sleeves

Make 2. With MC, cast on 17 sts. Work Full Square A and place 17 sts of row 34 on hold or bind off. With RS facing and cast-on edge at bottom, sl needle through 17

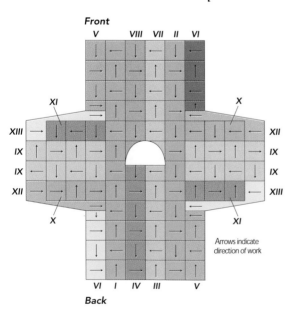

Front
V   VIII VII II   VI

XI

XIII   XII
IX   IX
IX   IX
XII   XIII

X

VI I   IV III   V

Back

Arrows indicate direction of work

garter loops along right side of square, ready to work a RS row. Work Square A, then B.

STRIP XII Underarm

Make 2. With MC, cast on 15 sts. **Rows 1–2** K with MC. **Rows 3–4** K with CC5. **Rows 5–32** Rep rows 1–4 a total of 7 times, AT SAME TIME, inc 1 st at beg of every 8th row 4 times—19 sts. **Rows 33–34** K with MC. **Rows 35–36** K2 MC, place rem 17 sts on hold; turn, k2 MC. **Rows 37–38** With another CC5, knit. **Rows 39–40** With MC, knit, inc 1 st at beg of row 40—3 sts. **Rows 41–68** Rep last 4 rows 7 times, AT SAME TIME, inc 1 st at beg of every 8th row 3 times—6 sts. **Rows 69–70** K with MC. **Rows 71–72** With another CC5, k and inc 1 st at beg of row 72—7 sts. **Rows 73–100** Rep last 4 rows 7 times, AT SAME TIME, inc 1 st at beg of every 8th row 3 times—10 sts. **Rows 101–102** K with MC. **Rows 103–104** K with MC and inc 1 st at beg of row 104—11 sts. **Rows 105–106** With another CC5, knit. **Rows 107–134** Rep last 4 rows 7 times, AT SAME TIME, inc 1 st at beg of row 108—12 sts. **Rows 135–136** K with MC. Place 12 sts on hold or bind off.

STRIP XIII Underarm

Make 2. Work as for Strip XII, reversing shaping as foll: Inc 1 st at end of every 8th row. On rows 35–36, cut yarn and place first 17 sts on hold. With MC, k2; turn, k2.

FINISHING

Block pieces. Join all strips, leaving underarm seams open.

Sleeve edging

With RS facing, smaller needles and MC, pick up and k64 sts around lower edge of sleeve. **Row 1** (WS) *K4, k2tog; rep from*, end k4—54 sts. **Rows 2, 4, 5** Purl. **Rows 3, 7** Knit. **Row 6** *K4, k2tog; rep from*—45 sts. **Rows 8–9** K with CC5. **Rows 10–11** K with MC. Rep last 4 rows 0 (1, 2) times. Cont with MC only: **Next row** Knit. **Next row** *P6, p2tog; rep from*, end p5—40 sts. Work 3 rows in rev St st. Bind off all sts. Work edging on 2nd sleeve.

Sew underarm seams. With RS facing, smaller needles, and MC, work trim and bands as foll:

Trim at lower edge

Beg at lower edge of left front, pick up and k41 (47, 51) sts to side seam, 82 (94, 102) sts along back, 41 (47, 51) sts along right front—164 (188, 204) sts. **Rows 1, 3, 5** (WS) Knit. **Rows 2, 4** Purl. Bind off all sts knitwise.

Neck trim

Beg at right front neck edge, pick up and k32 sts to shoulder, 44 sts along back and 32 sts to left front neck edge—108 sts. **Rows 1, 3, 5** (WS) Knit. **Rows 2, 4** Purl.

Place all sts on hold.

Button band

Beg at left front neck edge, pick up and k2 sts along trim, 85 sts along 5 squares, 3 sts along trim at lower edge—90 sts. **Rows 1, 3, 5** (WS) Knit. **Rows 2, 4** Purl. Cut yarn. Sl sts onto empty needle so that point of needle is at lower edge. With empty needle and MC, cast on 4 sts. Hold needle with 4 sts in left hand. Hold needle with 90 sts in right hand. **Work striped band: Row 1** Sl first st from right hand needle to left hand needle and with MC and right hand needle, k2tog, k3 (first st on hold connected to band). Turn. **Row 2** With MC, k4. **Row 3** With CC5, rep row 1. Turn. **Row 4** With CC5, k4. Rep Rows 1–4 until 1 st rem on right hand needle. Rep rows 1–2. Place 4 sts on hold.

Buttonhole band

Beg at lower edge of right front, pick up and k2 sts along trim, 85 sts along 5 squares, 2 sts along neck trim—89 sts. **Rows 1, 3, 5** (WS) Knit. **Rows 2, 4** Purl. Cut yarn. Point of needle is at lower edge. With MC, cast on 4 sts onto needle holding the 89 sts. **Work striped band: Row 1** With MC, k3, ssk (last st of band and first st on hold; see Appendix, p. 138). Turn. **Row 2** With MC, k4. **Row 3** With CC5, rep row 1. **Row 4** With CC5, k4. Rep rows 1–4 and end as for buttonband, AT SAME TIME, work 5 buttonholes by binding off 2nd and 3rd sts on rows 15, 49, 83, 117, 151 (on next row, cast them back on).

Neckband

Beg at right front neck edge and k 4 sts from band, 108 sts from neck, 4 sts from band—116 sts. K 1 row. [K 2 rows CC5, k 2 rows MC] twice, AT SAME TIME, make buttonhole at beg of 2nd CC5 stripe (bind off 3rd and 4th sts, cast on 2 sts on next row). With MC, k 1 row, p 2 rows, k1 row, p 1 row. Bind off all sts knitwise.

Front bands

Beg at lower edge of right front, pick up and k98 sts along buttonhole band. Work 4 rows in rev St st. Bind off all sts. In same way, work band along buttonband. Sew on buttons.

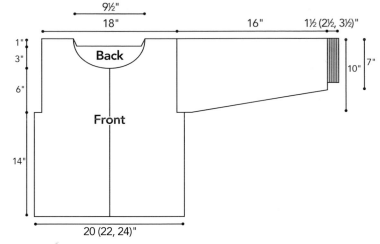

45

Simple fairisle

Fairisle—the color work

technique of using two

colors in a row, one carried

behind the other when not

in use—is a long-standing

method for combining

colors. It's also been used

(by Kaffe Fassett and

others) to include a variety

of yarns. For this book,

it seemed to me that the best

contribution I could make to

these glorious traditions

would be to simplify.

Both patterns in this section are based upon a very simple color pattern—a 6-stitch by 6-row repeat—that does not depend upon lights versus darks. This departs from popular traditions which usually have a more complex color repeat that relies upon lights versus darks for the stitch pattern to show. My offerings do not work this way: the complexity in the fabric is in the variety of colors and yarns.

The first garment, the child's version of *Caddy's Cardigan*, uses all one weight wool, and it is the only garment in this book for which I limited yarn choice. It was made long before work on this book began and when I assumed that working with a yarn stash meant sticking to the yarn on hand. (Silly me!) But the color range I chose was very broad (illustrating the option "pick a color and use anything you can stand next to it"), so I developed this simple color repeat to deal with the riot of color I faced.

This garment is included in the book—limited in fiber as it is—to offer contrast to the other multiple-fiber garments, and because you, too, might have lots of one lovely wool in your collection.

The adult's version of *Caddy's Cardigan* has some differences from the original garment. Although the color choices were guided by the same option, the result is much quieter. Also, a variety of fibers was included, but a main color is repeated throughout to integrate the different yarns used. (Working with several yarns in a fairisle pattern, a somewhat lighter weight yarn should be used in the same round with a somewhat heavier one: each will then be carried behind the other and balanced by it.)

To work fairisle, I have two preferences. One is to work in the round, so that I avoid purling with two colors. (The Appendix, p. 138 offers instructions for cutting and sewing the tubes for cardigan fronts and sleeves.) The other is to work with one color in each hand: the color in the right uses the "throw" or English method, and the color in the left uses the "pick" or Continental method. These are, however, only preferences. Work in the way you prefer.

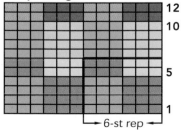

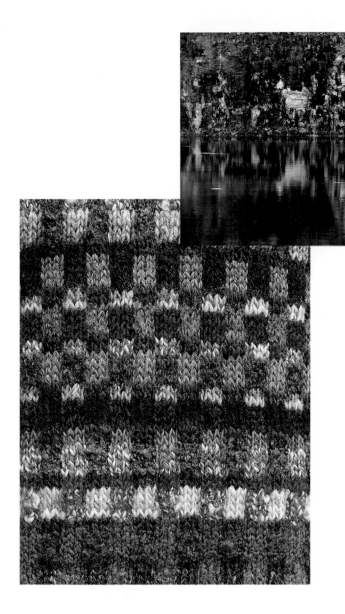

REPLACING COLOR
If you have finished a
piece and see a truly
terrible color choice,
you can replace this
color rather than rip out
and re-knit. Pick a new
color and duplicate
stitch over the first
row of the bad color,
following the process of
this yarn all the way to
the edge; now cut the
offending color out from
behind. Continue for
all following rows.

12
10

5

1

→ 6-st rep ←

12
10

5

1

→ 6-st rep ←

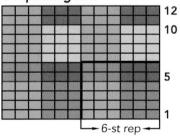

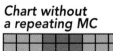

Caddy's Cardigan
child's version

Many years ago, long before this book, I saw lots of high quality DK wool in my collection, stuff too good not to be made into something. This became my first garment entirely from leftovers and was made for my 11-year-old daughter, Candace. The sweater was originally a pullover with ribbings at lower edges and neck, and within one year it was too small her! So I ripped off and replaced the edgings, sewed and cut the front open, put on front bands that covered all the rough edges, made FIMO buttons, and added crocheted button loops.

DIFFICULTY Intermediate

SIZES XS (S, M, L) to fit child's sizes 6 (8, 10, 12). Shown in size M.

FINISHED MEASUREMENTS Chest 30 (32, 34, 36)" Length 15 (17, 19, 21)"

GAUGE 23 sts and 26 rows to 4"/10cm in chart pat, using larger needles.

MATERIALS

Main color (MC) in DK weight yarn: 110 yds or approx one 1¾ oz/50g ball in navy to work edgings. If working chart pat with a repeating color, a 2nd ball is necessary.
Contrast colors (CC) in DK weight yarn: various colors. To work 2 chart rows/rnds for body: 10 (10.5, 11.5, 12)' lengths.
To work 4 chart rows/rnds for body: 20 (21.5, 22.5, 24)' lengths. (It takes twice the width of a row/rnd to work

one row/rnd. For example, a row 20" wide would take 40" of each CC.)
A. Sizes 3 and 5 (3.25 and 3.75mm) circular needles, both in 16"/40cm and 24"/60cm, *or size to obtain gauge.*
B. Size D/3 (3.00mm) crochet hook.
C. Seven ⅝" buttons in CCs.

STITCH PATTERN

Stranded fairisle worked in the round in St st from chart pat. As discussed earlier, work chart without a repeating MC if all fibers are the same. Work chart with a repeating MC if using a variety of fibers.

BODY

With size 3 (24") needle and MC, cast on 152 (162, 174, 184) sts. Place marker and join, being careful not to twist sts. **Work edging** P 6 rows, then k 1 row and inc 16 (18, 18, 20) times evenly across (in every 9th st)—168 (180, 192, 204) sts. Change to size 5 (24") needle. Work 6-st, 6-rnd rep of chart pat until piece measures 12½ (14½, 16, 18)" from beg, end at marker with chart row 6 (6, 2, 2).
Shape front neck
Cont chart pat, bind off 8 (9, 10, 11) sts, work around to marker. Turn, bind off 8 (9, 10, 11) sts, work around. Working back and forth in rows and cont chart pat as established, bind off 4 sts at beg of next 2 rows, 2 (3, 2, 3) sts at beg of next 2 rows, 1 st at beg of next 6 (6, 8, 8) rows—134 (142, 152, 160) sts. Work even until piece measures approx 15 (17, 19, 21)" from beg. Place all sts on hold. Place markers for armholes after 25 (26, 28, 29) sts on each side of center front. These are the right and left shoulder sts. The rem 84 (90, 96, 102) sts are for the back.

SLEEVES

With size 3 (16") needle and MC, cast on 29 (29, 33, 33) sts. Working back and forth in rows, work 4" in k2, p2 rib, end each RS row with k1 and beg each WS row with p1. **Next row** (WS) Purl and inc 13 (13, 9, 9) sts evenly across—42 sts. Change to size 5 (16") needle. Place marker, join and work 6-st, 6-row rep of chart pat, AT SAME TIME, inc 1 st each side of marker every other row 0 (0, 4, 8) times, every 4th row 10 (16, 16, 15) times, every 6th row 4 (1, 0, 0) times—70 (76, 82, 88)

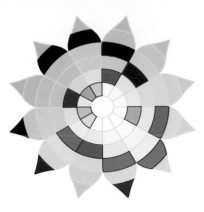

The Color Principles

- Pick a color you like (for this garment, I chose the medium intensity yellow-green), then use anything you can stand to see next to it.
- Use a minimum of ten colors.
- Combine colors randomly, paying no attention to lights versus darks.
- If using the chart without a repeating MC, pick a color for the neck, shoulder, and armhole edgings as dark as the darkest color used in the garment.
- If using the chart with a repeating MC, make this color as dark as or darker than the darkest color used in the garment, and use this color for all edgings.

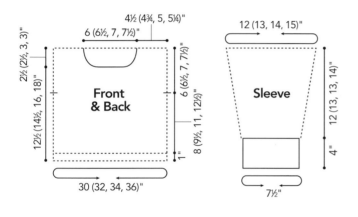

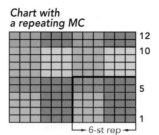

Chart with a repeating MC

← 6-st rep →

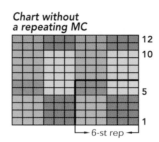

Chart without a repeating MC

← 6-st rep →

sts. Work even until piece measures 16 (17, 17, 18)" from beg, end with chart row 2 or 6. Place sts on hold.

FINISHING

Block pieces.

Neck and front openings

Baste a line down center front. Sew 2 tight lines of machine stitching along each side of center front. Cut along center line.

Armholes

Baste a line 6 (6½, 7, 7½)" down armhole between front shoulder sts and back sts. Sew 2 tight lines of machine stitching down each side of baste line for each armhole opening. Cut along center line.

Work trim

Work rev St st trim as foll: With RS facing and size 3 (24") needle, pick up and k sts as instructed. **Rows 1, 3, 5** (WS) Knit. **Rows 2, 4** Purl. Bind off all sts purlwise.

At shoulder With MC, k the rem sts along right front shoulder. Work trim. Tack bind-off row to first row, forming small roll. Graft sts of right back shoulder to just under roll of trim (see Grafting in Appendix, p. 138). In same way, work trim along left shoulder, then graft left back shoulder to front.

At armhole With MC, beg at underarm and pick up and k70 (76, 82, 88) sts inside line of machine stitching around armhole opening. Work trim. Covering raw edge, tack bind-off row to WS of opening.

At neck With MC, pick up and k88 (94, 98, 106) sts evenly around neck. Work trim. Covering edge, tack bind-off row to inside neck edge.

At front openings With approx 8½ (10, 11, 12½) yds of any color, beg at neck edge and pick up and k61 (71, 78, 89) sts inside line of machine stitching along left front opening. Work trim. Covering raw edge, tack bind-off row to WS of opening. In same way, beg at lower edge and work trim along right front.

Button loops

With crochet hook and MC, ch 22. Cut yarn and pull through last loop. Make 6 more chains. Using illustration as guide, form each chain into loops and sew to right front at regular intervals. Sew buttons on left front. Graft sleeve sts to inside of armhole, just under roll of trim. Sew cuff seams.

Button loops

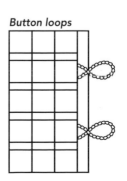

TECHNIQUE NOTES

1. Work stranded Fair Isle in the round in St st and in chart pat.
2. Except for front neck shaping, garment is worked in the round. Color changes occur at center front. Armhole and front openings are sewn and cut open. (See Appendix, p. 138.)

Caddy's Cardigan
adult's version

Once I started work on this book, it seemed natural to redo a little DK garment I had made from leftovers years ago. I had been teaching in Halifax, Nova Scotia, and did not have much of a yarn stash. So I went to a beautiful yarn shop and began to buy. This was the first time I went into a yarn shop to buy one ball of anything that appealed to me. What a liberating experience! This was also my first piece of two-handed fairisle inspired by my friend Sandi Minnes. What took me so long? (Sandi is shown wearing this sweater and with her son in the photo on p. 110.)

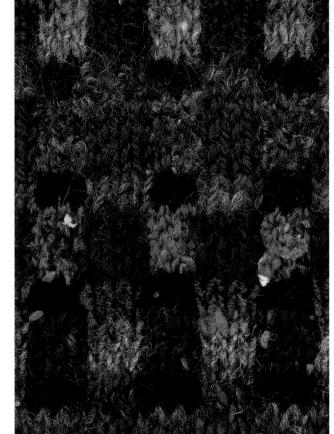

DIFFICULTY	Intermediate
SIZES	S (M, L). Shown in size M.
FINISHED MEASUREMENTS	Bust 40½, (45½, 50½)" Length 19 (21, 23)"
GAUGE	19 sts and 20 rows to 4"/10cm in St st using larger needles.

MATERIALS

Main color (MC) in worsted weight yarn: 170 yds or approx two 1¾oz/50g balls in black to work edgings. If working chart pat with a repeating color, another 100 (115, 130) yds, approx 1 (1, 2) 1¾oz/50g balls is necessary.
Contrast colors (CC) in DK to Aran weight yarns in greens, blue-greens, blues, blue-purples, purples, red-purples, and variegated yarns.
To work 2 chart rows/rnds for body: 14 (15.5, 17)' lengths.
To work 4 chart rows/rnds for body: 27.5 (30.5, 34)' lengths. (It takes twice the width of a row in each color

to work one row: for example, a row 20" wide would take 40" of each CC.)
A. Sizes 5 and 7 (3.75 and 4.5mm) circular needle, both in 16"/4cm and 24"/60cm, *or size to obtain gauge.*
B. Size E/4 (3.5mm) crochet hook.
C. Six ⅝" buttons in MC.

STITCH PATTERN

Stranded fairisle worked in the round in St st from chart pat. As discussed earlier, work chart without a MC if all fibers are the same. Work chart with a repeating MC if using a variety of fibers.

BODY

With size 5 (24") needle and MC, cast on 173 (195, 216) sts. Place marker and join, being careful not to twist sts.
Work edging P 6 rows, then k 1 row and inc 19 (21, 24) times evenly across (in every 9th st)—192 (216, 240) sts. Change to size 7 (24") needle. Work 6-st, 6-row rep of chart pat until piece measures 16 (18, 20)" from beg, end at marker with chart row 2.
Shape neck
Front neck Cont chart pat, bind off 7 (7, 8) sts, work around to marker. Turn work, bind off 7 (7, 8) sts, work around. Work back and forth in rows as foll: Cont chart pat, bind off 3 sts at beg of next 2 rows, 1 (2, 3) sts at beg of next 2 rows, 1 st at beg of next 6 rows—164 (186, 206) sts.
Back neck (RS) K34 (39, 43) sts, place marker (armhole), k36 (41, 45) sts, turn. *Bind off 1 st (right back neck), p in chart pat to front neck, turn. Work to back neck edge and rep from* once. Work 2 rows even. Place rem 68 (78, 86) sts on hold, keeping armhole marker in place. With RS facing, join yarn to right back neck and bind off 24 (26, 30) sts (center back neck), work to front neck edge, turn. Work 34 (39, 43) sts, place marker (armhole), work to back neck edge, turn. *Bind off 1 st (left back neck), work to end, turn. Work to back neck, turn and rep from* once. Work 2 rows even. Place rem sts on hold, keeping armhole marker in place.

SLEEVES

With size 5 (16") needle and MC, cast on 38 (42, 46) sts. Working back and forth in rows, work 3" in k1, p1 rib.
Next row (WS) Purl and inc 12 (14, 16) sts evenly across—50 (56, 62) sts. Change to size 7 (16") needle. Place marker, join and work 6-st, 6-row rep of chart pat,

The Color Principles

- Pick a color range you like, covering approximately one-half of the color wheel—for this garment, green to red-purple.
- Include variegated yarns that have any of this color range in them, even though they may include all sorts of other colors!
- Use a minimum of ten colors.
- Combine colors randomly, paying no attention to lights versus darks.
- If using the chart without a repeating MC, pick a color for the edgings as dark as the darkest color used in the garment.
- If using the chart with a repeating MC, make this color as dark as the darkest color used in the garment, and use this color for the edgings.
- The alternate colorway (shown in swatch on p. 47) was chosen similarly but beginning with warm colors (dark orange-reds) and ending with cool colors (blues). Varying intensities were included.

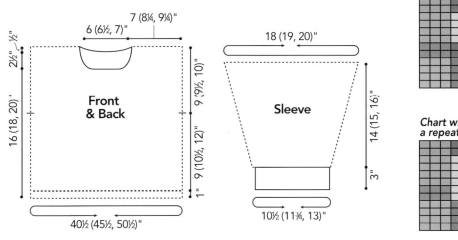

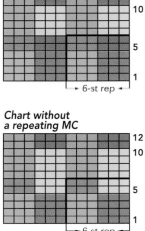

Chart with a repeating MC

Chart without a repeating MC

AT SAME TIME, inc 1 st each side of marker (working incs in chart pat) every 4th row 17 times—84 (90, 96) sts. Work even until piece measures 17 (18, 19)" from beg, end with chart row 2 or 6. Place sts on hold.

FINISHING

Block pieces.

Neck and front openings
Baste a line down center front. Sew 2 tight lines of machine stitching along each side of center front. Cut along center line.

Armholes
Baste a line 9 (9½, 10)" at marked point of armhole between front shoulder sts and back sts. Sew 2 tight lines of machine stitching down each side of baste line for each armhole opening. Cut along center line.

Work trim
Work rev St st trim as foll With RS facing and size 5 (24") needle, pick up and k sts as instructed. **Rows 1, 3, 5 (WS)** Knit. **Rows 2, 4** Purl. Bind off all sts purlwise.

At shoulder With MC, k the rem sts along right front shoulder. Work trim. Tack bind-off row to first row, forming small roll. Graft sts of right back shoulder to just under roll of trim (see Grafting in Appendix, p. 138). In

same way, work trim along left shoulder, then graft left back shoulder to front.

At armhole With MC, beg at underarm and pick up and k84 (90, 96) sts inside line of machine stitching around armhole opening. Work trim. Covering raw edge, tack bind-off row to WS of opening.

At neck With MC, pick up and k86 (90, 94) sts evenly around neck. Work trim. Covering edge, tack bind-off row to inside neck edge.

At front opening With MC, beg at neck edge and pick up and k86 (90, 94) sts inside line of machine stitching along left front opening. Work trim. Covering raw edge, tack bind-off row to WS of opening. In same way, beg at lower edge and work trim along right front.

Button loops
With crochet hook and MC, ch 12. Cut yarn and pull through last loop. Make 5 more chains. Using illustration as guide, form each chain into loops and sew to right front at regular intervals. Sew buttons on left front. Graft sleeve sts to inside of armhole, just under roll of trim. Sew cuff seams.

Button loops

TECHNIQUE NOTES
1. See notes for Caddy's cardigan (child's version), p. 49.
2. Buy FIMO in your favorite neutral color (black? brown? navy?) so you can always make buttons when you need them!

53

Not-your-usual intarsia

I love intarsia—the technique of using separate balls or strands of yarn for each area of color across a row—but not everybody does. Also, intarsia is usually worked in stockinette stitch—not the most accommodating to different yarn weights. So it was my challenge to take intarsia and make it work with different yarns. And it was also my challenge to design intarsia garments that might over-ride the reluctance of some knitters to work in this technique.

To draw a picture in knitting (for example, a forest floor) requires a separate ball or strand of yarn for each element (for example, for each leaf). These pictures are usually "drawn" in stockinette stitch. But stockinette stitch does not like different yarn weights: it reacts with bulges and hollows. How, then, to knit the Standing-in-a-pile-of-leaves sweater, since it would require a variety of yarns to "draw" this picture—or knit this garment? The solution was to use so *many* different yarns and to change them so *often* that the bulges and hollows would balance out in the end.

The result is a chart that looks like a nightmare! Just what knitters who dislike intarsia prefer to avoid! How could I encourage them to make this garment? By stressing the point that this chart is not meant to be followed exactly. Miss a color change by a stitch or two? Ignore it. Mis-read a color change? Change to whatever you like whenever you like. Run out of a strand of a color? Add anything in a similar color! The overall effect will not suffer from errors or omissions here or there, so go ahead and give it a shot. (And wouldn't it be nice if more of life was like this!)

Laurel's Jacket is also worked in intarsia—separate lengths of contrast color for each square. These regular square shapes are easy to work in intarsia: lengths can be pre-measured and pulled loose when they tangle. Also, regular shapes mean reading a chart is usually not necessary.

But here the stitch pattern is not simple stockinette. Instead, reverse stockinette stitches are off-set against squares of stockinette lace. The stitch patterns are off-set to help accommodate the different yarn weights used. The thinner yarns (which would fall into a hollow in stockinette stitch) are pushed out by reverse stockinette stitch. The thicker yarns (which would form bulges in plain stockinette stitch) are pulled back by the holes in the stockinette lace.

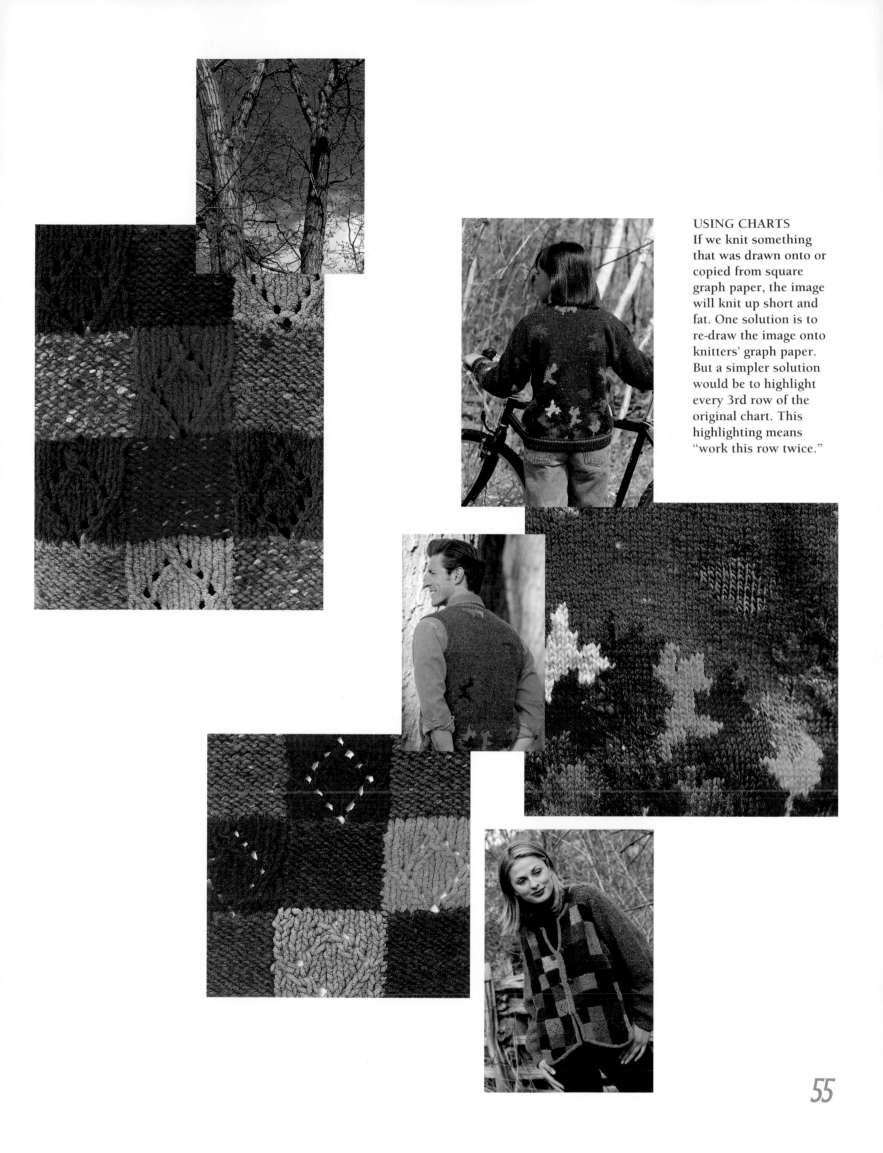

USING CHARTS

If we knit something that was drawn onto or copied from square graph paper, the image will knit up short and fat. One solution is to re-draw the image onto knitters' graph paper. But a simpler solution would be to highlight every 3rd row of the original chart. This highlighting means "work this row twice."

Standing-in-a-pile-of-leaves Pullover
child's version

In 1993, the Canadian movie 'Henry and Verlin' was made. It was directed by my stepson and based on stories by my late husband. After production, the producer asked me if I would knit sweaters as gifts for the principal actors. One was a very talented 11-year-old named Keegan MacIntosh, and it was for him that this garment was originally made. (See p. 62 for the continuation of this story.)

DIFFICULTY Intermediate

SIZES XS (S, M, L, XL) to fit child's sizes 4 (6, 8, 10, 12). Shown in size L.

FINISHED MEASUREMENTS Chest 30 (32, 34, 36, 38)"
Length 15 (16½, 17½, 19, 20½)"

GAUGE 22 sts and 31 rows to 4"/10cm in St st and chart pat using larger needles.

MATERIALS

Main color (MC) in DK weight yarn: 300 (420, 480, 540, 640) yds or approx 3 (3, 4, 4, 5) 1.75oz/50g balls in dark forest color.

Contrast colors (CC) in sport to worsted weight yarn: various lengths in leaf colors including yellows and yellow-oranges; oranges; red-oranges and reds; yellow-greens and greens; and browns.

A. Sizes 3 and 5 (3.25 and 3.75mm) needles, *or size to obtain gauge.*

B. Size 3 (3.25mm) circular needle, 16"/40cm.

C. One ⅝" button in a CC color.

BACK

With smaller needles and MC, cast on 81 (87, 93, 97, 103) sts. **Rib row 1** (RS) *K1, p1; rep from*, end k1. **Rib row 2** *P1, k1; rep from*, end p1. Rep rows 1–2 until rib is 2" from beg, end with a WS row. Change to larger needles. Beg and end as indicated by colored lines for your size, work chart pat (p. 58) until piece measures approx 14 (15½, 16½, 18, 19½)" from beg, end with a WS row. Mark center 23 (25, 27, 29, 31) sts.

Shape neck

Next row (RS) Work 29 (31, 33, 34, 36) sts, place marked sts on hold, join 2nd lengths of yarn and work to end. Cont chart pat and work each side separately as foll: Bind off from each neck edge 1 st twice. Work to top of chart. Piece measures approx 15 (16½, 17½, 19, 20½)" from beg. Bind off rem 27 (29, 31, 32, 34) sts each side.

FRONT

Work as for back through chart row 78 (90, 94, 98, 108). **Divide for front placket: Row 79 (91, 95, 99, 109)** (RS) Work 39 (42, 45, 47, 50) sts, bind off next 3 sts, join separate lengths of yarn and work to end. Working each side at same time, cont chart pat until piece measures 12½ (14, 15, 16½, 18)" from beg, end with a WS row.

Shape neck

Bind off from each neck edge 5 (6, 6, 6, 6) sts once, 2 sts 1 (1, 1, 2, 2) times, 1 st 5 (5, 6, 5, 6) times. Work even until piece measures same as back to shoulder. Bind off all sts.

SLEEVES

With smaller needles and MC, cast on 41 (43, 43, 45, 47) sts. Work 2" in k1, p1 rib as for back, end with RS row. Change to larger needles and p 1 row, inc 6 (6, 10, 10, 10) sts evenly across—47 (49, 53, 55, 57) sts. Beg and end as indicated by colored lines for your size, work in chart pat, AT SAME TIME, inc 1 st each side every 4th row 12 (14, 15, 17, 19) times—71 (77, 83, 89, 95) sts.

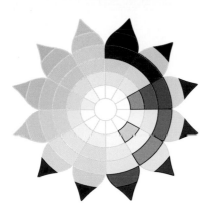

The Color Principles

- MC is worked in a dark color appropriate for the forest—green, blue-green, blue, brown, gray, or black; for this garment, MC is dark blue-green.
- Tweedy yarns work particularly well as MC.
- CCs are worked in leaf colors in light-medium to dark intensity: yellows and yellow-oranges; oranges; red-oranges and reds; yellow-greens and greens; and browns.

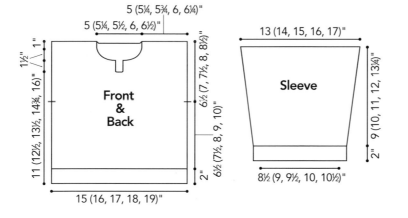

Work even in chart pat until piece measures 11 (12, 13, 14, 15¼)" from beg. Bind off all sts.

FINISHING

Block pieces. Sew shoulder seams.

Neckband

With circular needle and MC, beg at right front neck and pick up and k99 (101, 103, 105, 107) sts evenly around neck edge, including sts on hold. Place marker, join and work 5 rnds in k1, p1 rib. P 1 rnd for turning ridge, then work 4 rnds more in rib. Bind off all sts loosely. Fold neckband at turning ridge and tack to WS.

Placket edging

With smaller needles and MC, beg at right front lower edge of placket and pick up and k19 sts to top of neckband. Work 7 rows in k1, p1 rib. Bind off in rib. In same way, beg at top of neckband at left edge and pick up and k19 sts to placket opening. Work 7 rows in k1, p1 rib, making 3-row buttonhole in 4th st on rows 3–5 (see Appendix, p. 138). Bind off all sts.

Sew lower edges of placket to front. Sew on button. Place markers 6½ (7, 7½, 8, 8½)" down from shoulders on front and back. Sew top of sleeves between markers. Sew side and sleeve seams.

TECHNIQUE NOTES

1. Garment is worked in stockinette stitch (k on RS, p on WS) intarsia from the chart on p. 58. Separate lengths of MC and CC are used for each area of work.

2. Be sure to twist yarns at color change to avoid holes.

3. For the bottom band and cuff ribbing, beg with MC, then switch to CCs for subsequent rows. Remember that it takes 3 times the width of the row to work 1 row.

- A leaf shown in one color with a dark line through it means that the leaf can be worked in one color or two versions of the same color.
- If your color runs out before leaf is done, just continue working in an alternate yarn within the same color group.

Standing-in-a-pile-of-leaves pullover (adult and child)

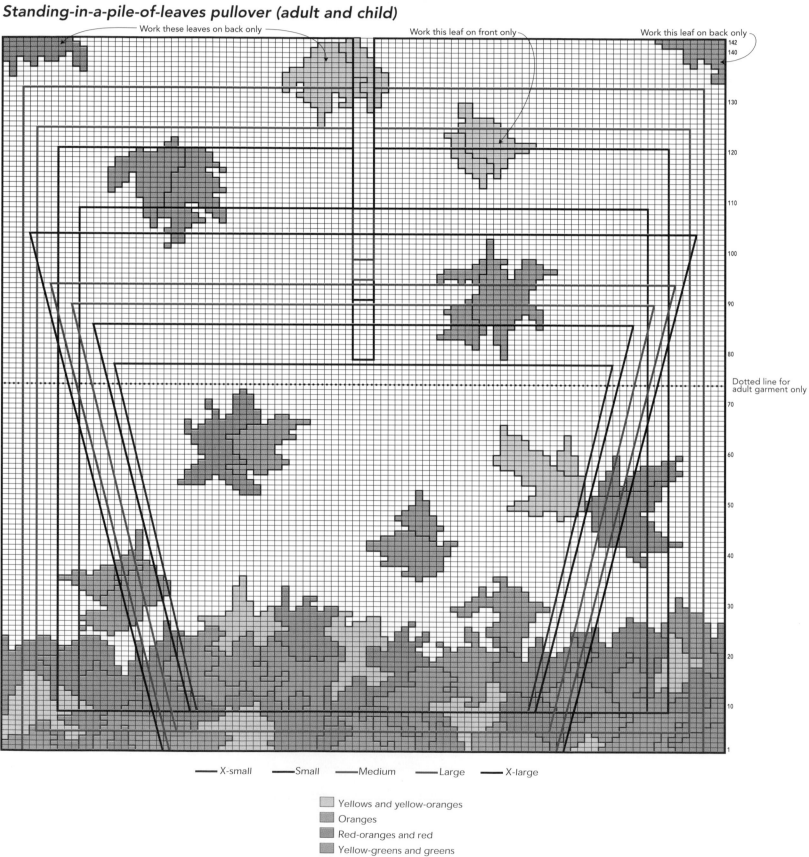

Work these leaves on back only

Work this leaf on front only

Work this leaf on back only

142
140

130

120

110

100

90

80

Dotted line for adult garment only

70

60

50

40

30

20

10

1

——X-small ——Small ——Medium ——Large ——X-large

- Yellows and yellow-oranges
- Oranges
- Red-oranges and red
- Yellow-greens and greens
- Browns
- MC

58

Standing-in-a-pile-of-leaves Pullover
adult's version

DIFFICULTY   Intermediate

SIZES   XS (S, M, L, XL). No model shown.

FINISHED   Chest 38 (41, 44, 46, 50)"
MEASUREMENTS   Length 22 (23½, 25½, 27, 28½)"

GAUGE   17 sts and 23 rows to 4"/10cm in
chart pat using larger needles.

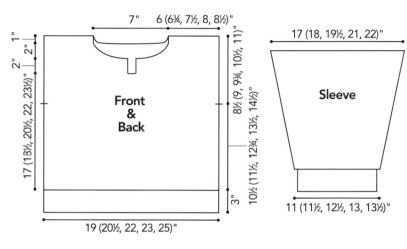

MATERIALS

Main color (MC) in Aran weight yarn: 500 (550, 660, 750, 850) yds or approx 6 (7, 8, 9, 10) 1¾oz/50g balls in dark forest color.

Contrast colors (CC) in DK to Aran weight yarn: various lengths in leaf colors including yellows and yellow-oranges; oranges; orange-reds and reds; yellow-greens and greens; and browns.

A. Sizes 6 and 8 (4 and 5mm) needles, *or size to obtain gauge.*

A. Size 6 (4mm) circular needle, 16" (40cm).

C. One ¾" button in a CC.

BACK

Work as for Child's Pullover, working 3" in rib and working 10 (10, 10, 6, 6) plain rows at dotted line in chart. Cont chart pat until piece measures 21 (22½, 24½, 26, 27½)" from beg, end with a WS row. Mark center 25 sts.

Shape neck

Cont chart pat, work to marked sts and place them on hold, join 2nd lengths of yarn and work to end. Working both sides at same time with separate yarns, bind off 1 st at each neck edge twice. Work even until piece measures 22 (23½, 25½, 27, 28½)" from beg. Bind off rem 26 (29, 32, 34, 37) sts each side.

FRONT

Work as for back through chart row 78 (90, 94, 98, 108) (working extra rows at dotted line on chart). Piece measures approx 17 (18½, 20½, 22, 23½)" from beg. **Divide for front placket: Row 79 (91, 95, 99, 109)** (RS) Work 39 (42, 45, 47, 50) sts, place next 3 sts on hold, join separate lengths of yarn and work to end. Working each side at same time, cont chart pat until piece measures 19 (20½, 22½, 24, 25½)" from beg, end with a WS row.

Shape neck

Bind off from each neck edge 6 sts once, 2 sts once, 1 st 5 times. Work even until piece measures same as back to shoulder. Bind off rem 26 (29, 32, 34, 37) sts each side.

SLEEVES

Work as for Child's Pullover, p. 56, working 3" in rib and working 12 plain rows at dotted line on chart.

FINISHING

Block pieces. Sew shoulder seams.

Neckband and front placket

With RS facing, circular needle, and MC, pick up and k101 sts evenly around neck edge. Complete as for Child's Pullover. Work placket as for Child's Pullover. Place markers 8½ (9, 9¾, 10½, 11)" down from shoulders on front and back. Sew top of sleeves between markers. Sew side and sleeve seams. Sew on button.

TECHNIQUE NOTES

See notes for Child's Pullover, p. 57. Unless otherwise indicated, foll the numbers given in the Child's Pullover pattern, pp. 56-57. Work from the chart on p. 58. The different gauges result in the different sizes.

Standing-in-a-pile-of-leaves Vest

To continue the story begun on p. 56, the second principal actor for the movie was a man— a very large man with a 56" chest! I was under a bit of a time constraint for these garments, so the big guy, Canadian actor Gary Farmer, got a vest. These garments allow you to use all the strong and warm colors in your collection but not near the face where they are unflattering to most of us.

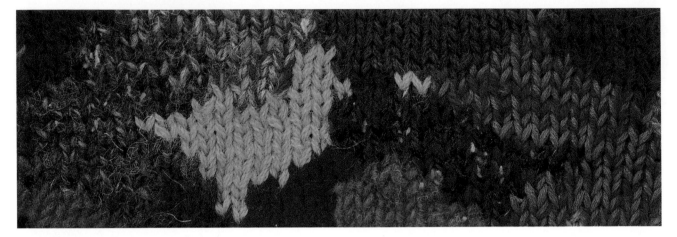

DIFFICULTY	Advanced
SIZES	S (M, L, XL). Shown in size M.
FINISHED MEASUREMENTS	Chest 42 (46, 50, 54)" Length 23 (24, 25, 26)"
GAUGE	17 sts and 23 rows to 4"/10cm in St st and chart pat using larger needles.

MATERIALS

Main color (MC) in Aran weight yarn: 400 (440, 520, 580) yds or approx 5 (5, 6, 7) 1¾oz/50g balls in dark forest color.

Contrast colors (CC) in DK to Aran weight yarn: various lengths in leaf colors including yellows and yellow-oranges; oranges; orange-reds and reds; yellow-greens and greens; and browns.

A. Sizes 6 and 8 (4 and 6mm) needles, *or size to obtain gauge.*

B. Five ¾" buttons in MC.

BACK

With smaller needles and MC, cast on 90 (98, 106, 114) sts. Work 8 rows in k1, p1 rib. Change to larger needles. Beg and end as indicated for your size and working 0 (6, 8, 16) extra rows in MC only as indicated on chart (p. 64), work in chart pat until piece measures 13 (14, 14, 15)" from beg, end with a WS row.

Shape armhole

Cont chart pat, bind off 9 sts at beg of next 2 rows. Dec 1 st each side every other row 6 (8, 9, 9) times—60 (64, 70, 78) sts. Work even in chart pat until armhole measures 9 (9, 10, 10)", end with WS row. Mark center 24 sts.

Shape shoulder and neck

Cont pat, bind off 5 (6, 7, 8) sts, work to marked sts. Turn, bind off 1 st (back neck), work to end. Rep from once. Bind off rem sts. With RS facing and MC, join yarn and bind off center 24 sts, work to end. At shoulder edge, bind off 5 (6, 7, 8) sts twice, AT SAME TIME, bind off 1 st at neck edge twice. Bind off rem sts.

RIGHT FRONT

With smaller needles and MC, cast on 67 (73, 79, 85) sts. **Row 1** (RS) Work 32 (36, 38, 42) sts in k1, p1 rib; k1 (0, 1, 0), place marker (pm), k1 (center st), pm, k1 (0, 1, 0), work rem 32 (36, 38, 42) sts in p1, k1 rib. **Row 2** P1, inc 1 in next st, work rib as established to 2 sts before marker, work 2 tog, p1 (center st), work 2 tog, work rib as established to last 2 sts, inc 1 in next st, p1. Work 5 rows more in rib as established, working row 2 every WS row. Change to larger needles. **Row 8** (WS) Rep row 2—67 (73, 79, 85) sts. Cut yarn. Sl sts to center st.
Shape point and dec to 45 (49, 53, 57) sts as foll: **Beg Right Front chart: Row 1** K1 from chart (center st); turn. **Row 2** P1, p2tog, p1; turn. **Row 3** K to break between sts of garment piece and rib, k2tog, k1; turn. **Row 4** P to break, p2tog, p1. Rep rows 3–4 until all sts from rib have been brought into garment piece. Cont, foll chart pat on p. 64 until piece measures same as back to armhole, end with a RS row.

Shape armhole and neck

Next row (WS) Bind off 9 sts, work to end. Dec 1 st at armhole every other row 6 (8, 9, 9) times, AT SAME TIME, dec 1 st at neck edge every 4th row 14 times. Work even until armhole measures same as back to shoulder, end with a RS row.

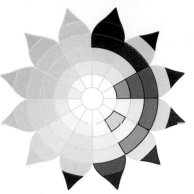

The Color Principles
- MC is worked in a dark color appropriate for the forest—green, blue-green, blue, brown, gray, or black; for this garment, MC is dark brown.
- Tweedy yarns work particularly well as MC.
- CCs are worked in leaf colors in light-medium to dark intensities: yellows and yellow-oranges; oranges; orange-reds and reds; yellow-greens and greens; plus browns.

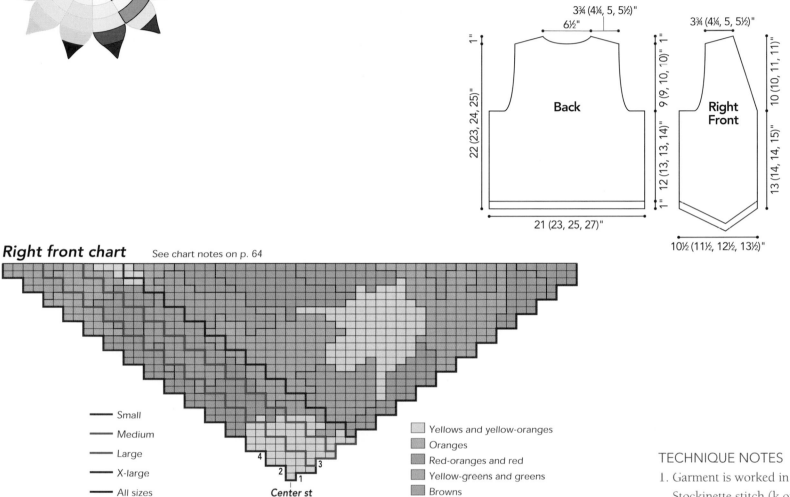

Right front chart   *See chart notes on p. 64*

Small
Medium
Large
X-large
All sizes

4
2
1
3
Center st

- Yellows and yellow-oranges
- Oranges
- Red-oranges and red
- Yellow-greens and greens
- Browns

Shape shoulder
At shoulder edge, bind off 5 (6, 7, 8) sts twice. Bind off rem sts.

LEFT FRONT
Work as for right front, reversing all shaping.

FINISHING
Block pieces. Sew shoulder seams.

Button band
With RS facing, smaller needles, and MC, beg at lower edge of right front and pick up and k3 sts for every 4 rows along front to beg of V neck shaping, work k1, yo, k1 in st at point of V, 5 sts for every 6 rows along V-neck to shoulder, 5 sts along back neck shaping, 1 st for every bound-off st to center back. Work 6 rows in k1, p1 rib. Bind off all sts. Sew 5 buttons to band, spacing evenly between point of V and lower edge.

Buttonhole band
With RS facing, smaller needles, and MC, beg at center back neck and pick up and k1 st for every bound-off st at center back, 5 sts along left back neck shaping, 5 sts for every 6 rows along V-neck, work k1, yo, k1 in st at point of V, 3 sts for every 4 rows along left front to lower edge. Work 5 rows in k1, p1 rib, working five 3-row button-holes (see Appendix, p. 138) opposite buttons on rows 2–4. Bind off all sts. Sew bands tog at center back.

Armbands
With RS facing, smaller needles, and MC, beg at under-arm and pick up and k 1 st for every bound-off st and 3 sts for every 4 rows around armhole edge. Work 4 rows in k1, p1 rib. Bind off all sts.
Sew side seams, including armbands.

TECHNIQUE NOTES
1. Garment is worked in Stockinette stitch (k on RS, p on WS) intarsia from the charts here and on page 64. Separate strands of MC and CC are used for each area of work.
2. Be sure to twist yarns at color change to avoid holes.
3. For the bottom band ribbing, beg with MC, then switch to CCs for subsequent rows. Remember that it takes 3 times the width of the row to work 1 row.

- A leaf shown in one color with a dark line through it means that the leaf can be worked in one color or two versions of the same color.
- If your color runs out before leaf is done, just continue working in an alternate yarn within the same color group.

Standing-in-a-pile-of-leaves vest

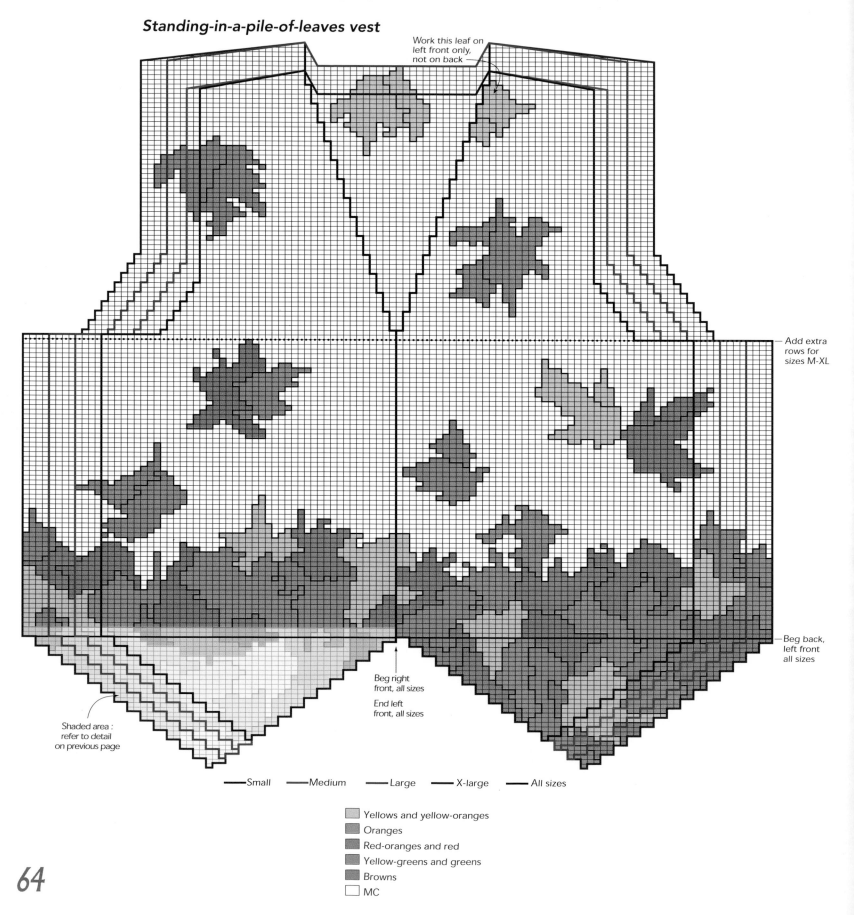

Work this leaf on left front only, not on back

Add extra rows for sizes M-XL

Beg back, left front all sizes

Shaded area : refer to detail on previous page

Beg right front, all sizes

End left front, all sizes

—Small —Medium —Large —X-large —All sizes

- Yellows and yellow-oranges
- Oranges
- Red-oranges and red
- Yellow-greens and greens
- Browns
- MC

Laurel's Jacket

About eight years ago, I knit the brown version of this garment. The precious chenilles and wool tweeds in my collection called to me, and the result was for many years, my favorite sweater. Then about five years ago, I knit the fuchsia version for my best friend, Laurel. I did it while my husband was very ill (and was so distracted that I forgot to work the eyelet st pat in the sleeves). I gave it to her for her 50th birthday, the day after he died. This garment has some pretty powerful associations.

DIFFICULTY	Advanced
SIZES	S (M, L, XL). Model is in size L.
FINISHED MEASUREMENTS	Bust 40 (45, 50, 55)" Length 20 (22½, 22½, 25)"
GAUGE	14 sts and 24 rows to 4"/10cm in St st using chunky weight yarn and largest needles. Or, 18 sts and 28 rows to 4"/10cm in St st using Aran weight yarn and 2nd largest needles.

MATERIALS

Chunky weight (fuchsia) version

Sleeve color in chunky weight wool tweed yarn: 350 yds or approx three 3½oz/100g balls in red-purple.

Trim color in Aran or chunky weight wool tweed yarn: 150 yds in black.

Contrast colors (CC) in chunky weight cotton chenilles (CC1) and in Aran to chunky weight wool tweeds (CC2): 3-yd lengths in light to dark intensity red-purples, purples, blue-purples, blues, and blue-greens. (Both sleeve and trim color are also used as CC2.) Total length required for each CC is 175 (225, 240, 300) yds.

A. Sizes 6, 7 and 8 (4, 4.5 and 5mm) needles, *or size to obtain gauge.*

B. Size H/8 (5.00mm) crochet hook.

C. Eight ⅝" button in trim color.

Aran weight (brown) version

Sleeve color in Aran weight wool tweed yarn: 350 (350, 400, 400) yds or approx 4 (4, 5, 5) 1¾oz/50g balls in brown.

Trim color may be any dark CC2: 100 yds required.

Contrast colors (CC) in chunky weight cotton chenilles (CC1) and in Aran weight wool tweeds (CC2): 3-yd lengths in light to dark intensity colors from most of the color wheel. (Both sleeve and trim color are also used as CC2.) Total length required for each CC is 175 (225, 240, 300) yds.

A. Sizes 6 and 7 (4 and 4.5mm) needles, *or size to obtain gauge.*

B. Size G/6 (4.50mm) crochet hook.

C. Eight ⅝" buttons in sleeve color. (**Note** Although I used only six as shown in the photo, I recommend eight.)

STITCH PATTERNS

Eyelet squares – Full pattern

Worked over 9 sts and 14 rows with CC1 (a heavier yarn than CC2 if using 2 distinct yarn weights).

Row 1 (RS) K4, yo, ssk, k3. **Row 2 and all WS rows** P9. **Row 3** K2, k2tog, yo, k1, yo, ssk, k2. **Row 5** K1, k2tog, yo, k3, yo, ssk, k1. **Row 7** K2tog, yo, k5, yo, ssk. **Row 9** K2, yo, ssk, k1, k2tog, yo, k2. **Row 11**: K3, yo, sl 1, k2tog, psso, yo, k3. **Row 13** Rep row 1. **Row 14** P9.

Rev St st squares

Worked over 5 or 9 sts and 14 rows with CC2 (a lighter yarn than CC1 if using two distinct yarn weights).

Row 1 (RS) Knit. **Row 2 and all WS rows** Knit. **Rows 3, 5, 7, 9, 11, 13** Purl. **14** Knit.

Eyelet lace (optional st pat for sleeves)

(Worked over 10 sts and 16 rows with sleeve color).

Row 1 (RS) Knit. **Row 2 and all WS rows** Purl. **Row 3** K2, yo, ssk, k6. **Row 5** K2tog, yo, k1, yo, ssk, k5. **Row 7** Knit. **Row 9** K7, yo, ssk, k1. **Row 11** K5, k2tog, yo, k1, yo, ssk. **Row 15** Knit. **Row 16** Purl.

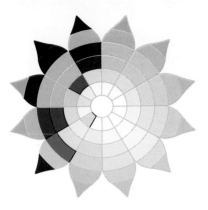

The Color Principles: fuchsia version
- Sleeve is worked in a medium-intensity color.
- Trim is worked in the darkest yarn used throughout.
- CCs are light to dark intensity, all from the cool side of the color wheel.

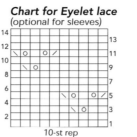

Chart for Eyelet squares (full square)

9-st rep

Chart for Eyelet lace (optional for sleeves)

10-st rep

☐ k on RS, p on WS
⊙ Yo
⟋ K2tog
⟍ SSK
△ Sl 1, k2tog, psso

TECHNIQUE NOTES
1. Twist yarns at color changes to avoid holes.
2. Work selvage sts each side in St st. Selvage sts are not included in measurements.
3. Sleeves may be worked in St st or in Eyelet lace stitch pat.
4. Lower edge trim on brown version is shown as rev St st, but the pattern is written for rib. (The rolled edge did not work well with the points. I do not recommend it and do not offer instructions for it. I wish I had enough brown tweed yarn to replace it!)
5. This garment could be made with CC1 and CC2 as any contrasting fibers or textures: nubbly wool with smooth wool; cotton with mohair; mohair with silk blend.

BACK
With size 6 needles and trim color, cast on 73 (83, 91, 101) sts. Work 1" in k1, p1 rib. Change to size 7 needles. P 1 row and inc 1 (0, 1, 0) sts in middle of row—74 (83, 92, 101) sts. **Beg pats: Row 1** (RS) K1 (selvage) *work 9 sts in rev St st square pat, 9 sts in Eyelet square pat; rep from* across and **for sizes M, XL only**, end with 9 sts in rev St st square, **for all sizes**, k1 (selvage). Work through pat row 14, then alternate pats by beg with Eyelet square pat. Work even until 4 (5, 5, 6) squares have been worked from beg, end with pat row 14.

Shape armhole
For size S *Dec 1 st each side every RS row 3 times, work 1 RS row even, rep from* 4 times, dec 1 st each side next RS row, work 1 WS row—42 sts.

For size M *Dec 1 st each side every RS row 9 times, work 1 RS row even, rep from* once, dec 1 st each side next RS row, work 1 WS row even—45 sts.

For size L Dec 1 st each side every RS row 21 times—50 sts.

For size XL *Dec 1 st each side every RS row 7 times, then dec 1 st each side next WS row; rep from* twice—53 sts.

For all sizes Bind off all sts.

RIGHT FRONT
For sizes M, XL only, after point shaping is completed, work half squares at center front as foll: **Row 1** (RS) K5. **Row 2 and all WS rows** P5. **Row 3** K1, yo, ssk, k2. **Row 5** K2, yo, ssk, k1. **Row 7** K3, yo, ssk. **Row 9** K1, k2tog, yo, k2. **Row 11** K2tog, yo, k3. **Row 13** K5. **Row 14** P5.

With size 6 needles and trim color, cast on 55 (63, 69, 75) sts. **Row 1** (RS) Work 26 (30, 34, 36) sts in k1, p1 rib; k 1 (1, 0, 1), place marker (pm), k1 (center st), pm, k1 (1, 0, 1), beg with p1 and work rem 26 (30, 34, 36) sts in p1, k1 rib. **Row 2** P1, inc 1 in next st, rib as established to 2 sts before marker, work 2 tog, p1 (center st), work 2 tog, rib as established to last 2 sts, inc 1 in next st, p1. **Rows 3–6** Rep Rows 1–2, changing to size 7 needles after row 5—55 (63, 69, 75) sts. Cut yarn. Sl sts to center st.

Shape point and dec to 38 (43, 47, 52) sts as foll: **Beg Right Front chart: Row 1** Beg with row 1, work from right front chart and k1 (center st, work from chart); turn. **Row 2** P1, p2tog, p1; turn. **Row 3** Work to break between sts of garment and rib, k2tog, k1; turn. **Row 4** Work to break, p2tog, p1. Rep rows 3–4 until 3 (4, 4, 4) sts rem from rib at each end, end with RS row. **For size S only** (WS) Work to break, p2tog, p1; turn, work to break, k3—38 sts. **For sizes M, L only** (WS) Work to break, p2tog, p2; turn, work to break, k2tog, k2—43 (47) sts. **For size XL only** (WS) Work to break p2tog, p2; turn, work to break, k4—52 sts rem. Cont in st pats as established (working half squares pat at center front for sizes M and XL) until piece measures same as back to armhole. Shape armhole as for back—22 (24, 26, 28) sts. Bind off all sts.

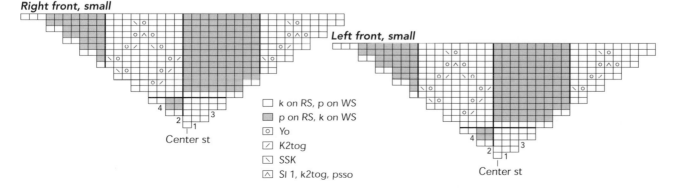

Right front, small

4 3
2 1
Center st

Left front, small

4 3
2 1
Center st

☐ k on RS, p on WS
▦ p on RS, k on WS
⊙ Yo
⟋ K2tog
⟍ SSK
△ Sl 1, k2tog, psso

67

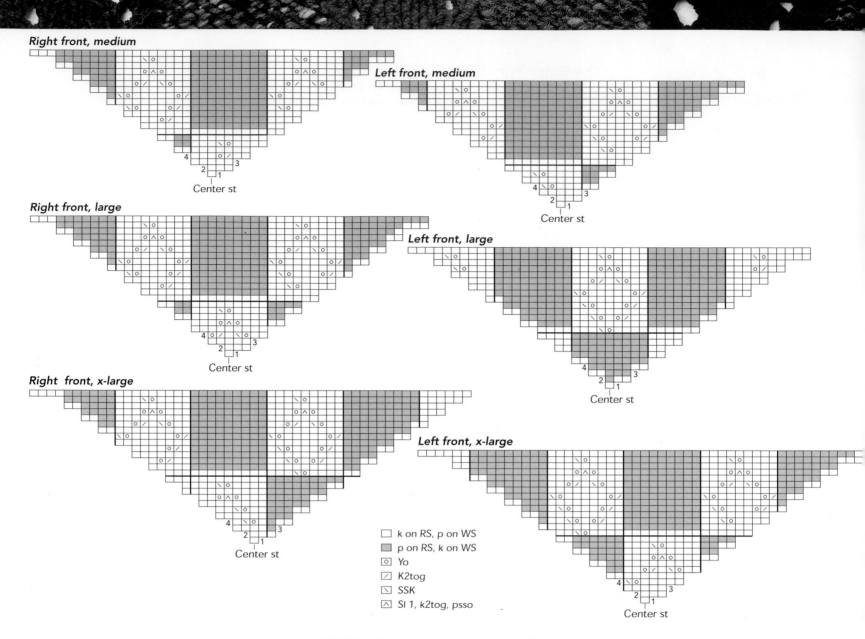

Right front, medium

Left front, medium

Center st

Right front, large

Left front, large

Center st

Center st

Right front, x-large

Left front, x-large

Center st

Center st

☐ k on RS, p on WS
▨ p on RS, k on WS
⊙ Yo
☑ K2tog
◣ SSK
△ Sl 1, k2tog, psso

LEFT FRONT

Work as for right front, working from left front chart and reversing all shaping. **For sizes M, XL only** after point shaping is complete, work half squares pat at center front as foll: **Row 1** K5. **Row 2 and all WS rows** P5. **Row 3** K2, k2tog, yo, k1. **Row 5** K1, k2tog, yo, k2. **Row 7** K2tog, yo, k3. **Row 9** K2, yo, ssk, k1. **Row 11** K3, yo, ssk. **Row 13** K5. **Row 14** P5.

RIGHT SLEEVE & YOKE

(using chunky weight yarn)

With size 7 needles and trim color, cast on 29 (31, 33, 35) sts. Work 3" in k1, p1 rib. Change to size 8 needles and sleeve color. P 1 row and inc 7 (5, 3, 1) sts evenly across—36 sts. Work in St st or Eyelet lace pat as desired, AT SAME TIME, inc 1 st each side every 4th row 14 times—64 sts. Work even until piece measures 18 (19, 20, 21)" from beg, end with a WS row.

Shape armhole and yoke

Dec 1 st each side of every RS row 9 times, then dec 1 st each side of next WS row; rep from once—24 sts. Work 2 (2½, 3, 3½)" even, end with WS row.

Shape front neck

K12; turn, bind off 4 sts (neck edge), work to end. Bind off at neck edge 2 sts once, 1 st 6 times. Fasten off.

Shape back neck

With RS facing, join yarn to back neck, ready to work RS row. Bind off 1 st at neck edge twice. Work even on rem 10 sts until piece measures 4" from beg of back neck shaping. Place sts on hold.

RIGHT SLEEVE & YOKE

(using Aran weight yarn)

With size 6 needles and sleeve color, cast on 35 (37, 39, 41) sts. Work 3" in k1, p1 rib. Change to size 7 needles and sleeve color. P 1 row, inc 9 (7, 5, 3) sts evenly across—44 sts. Work in St st or Eyelet lace pat as desired, AT SAME TIME, inc 1 st each side every 6th row 18 times—80 sts. Work even until piece measures 18 (19, 20, 21)" from beg, end with a WS row.

Shape armhole and yoke

Dec 1 st each side of every RS row 5 times, then dec 1 st each side of next WS row once; rep from 3 times—32 sts. Work 2 (2½, 3, 3½)" even, end with WS row.

The Color Principles: brown version

- Sleeve is worked in a medium-intensity color.
- Trim should be worked in the darkest yarn used throughout.
- CCs are light to dark intensity, all from one side of the color wheel (yellow to purple) with the inclusion of a complementary color (blue-green).

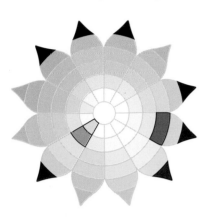

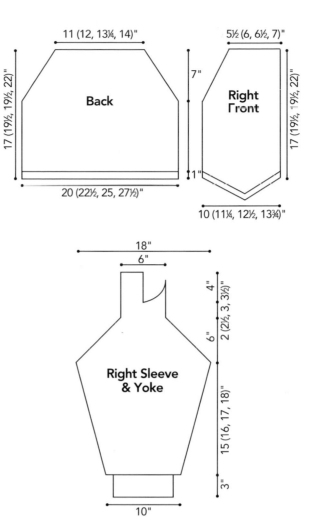

Shape front neck

K15; turn, bind off 5 sts (neck edge) work to end. Bind off at neck edge 3 sts once, 1 st 7 times. Fasten off.

Shape back neck

With RS facing, join yarn to back neck, ready to work RS row. Bind off 1 st at neck edge twice. Work even on rem 13 sts until piece measures 4" from beg of back neck shaping. Place sts on hold.

LEFT SLEEVE & YOKE

Work as for right sleeve (using chunky or Aran weight yarn), reversing neck shaping.

FINISHING

Block pieces. Sew sleeves to front and back, end front neck 2" from center front edge, end back at center. Graft yokes tog at center back. Sew side and sleeve seams.

Neckband

With RS facing, smallest needles, and trim color, pick up and k70 sts evenly around neck edge. Work 1" in rev St st. Bind off. Tack bound-off edge to picked-up edge to form roll.

Front bands

With RS facing, smallest needles, and trim color, pick up and k3 sts for every 4 rows along each front edge, including neckband. Work 1" in rev St st. Bind off. Tack bound-off edge to picked-up edge.

Button loops

With crochet hook and trim color, make a total of four 4" chains. Form each chain into a figure 8 and sew to right front edge for button loops. Sew 4 buttons to right front and to left front to match placement of loops.

Tweed stitch squares

There are stitch patterns

in knitting dictionaries

called "bi-color."

Their distinguishing feature

is that they are simply

stripes: two rows of color A,

two rows of color B.

Most wonderful are the ones

for which every wrong side

row is purl!

These stitch patterns involve

some manipulation of a knit

stitch (by slipping a stitch,

knitting into the stitch

below, or by purling),

so simple stripes produce a

fabric which does not look

like stripes. This process

also produces fabric which

integrates colors and

accommodates different

yarn weights.

My favorite bi-color stitch pattern is tweed stitch. This was the first stitch pattern I explored when I began to work on this book. It is simple to work but produces a beautiful fabric from a diverse collection of yarns and colors. What more could I ask?

Before beginning the patterns in this section, try a small swatch in just two colors of yarn. It will familiarize you with the stitch pattern and also serve as a gauge swatch. Choose your main color (MC), perhaps a darker color, and choose a contrast color (CC). Work as follows over any even number of stitches: **Row 1** With MC, k1, *k1, sl 1 purlwise with yarn in front, rep from* to last st, k1. **Row 2** With MC, purl. **Row 3** With CC, k1, *sl 1 purlwise with yarn in front, k1, rep from* to last st, k1. **Row 4** With CC, purl. Repeat these 4 rows.

The stitch pattern is quite wonderful just worked in stripes. You could work any or all of the tweed stitch squares garments that follow in simple stripes—working two rows of every four in main color but changing contrast colors only at the beginnings of rows. Use only one contrast color or as many as your heart desires!

I began my exploration of tweed stitch with stripes but became really excited when I began working the contrast colors in squares.

The squares are worked as intarsia motifs—separate two yard lengths for each contrast color across the row—but this work is quite easy, a perfect "learn-to-love" intarsia project. Why? Because two of every four rows are worked entirely in main color; this means *half* the garment is not intarsia at all. Secondly, the motifs are simple squares; there is no graph to follow. Thirdly, each square takes two yards of contrast color; this is an easy length to measure and cut, to dis-entangle from other contrast colors, and you're done with it before serious tangling can occur.

CHOOSING STITCHES
Collect knitting dictionaries! When choosing a stitch pattern, I look for those in which every other row is purl. Why sort out patterns on wrong side rows if we don't have to? I also choose those that I will be able to understand and anticipate easily. It's not fun to be tied to instructions for the duration of a project.

71

Topher's Pullover
DK version

Five years ago my daughter asked me to knit a sweater for someone special. She was 16 and the guy, Topher, was turning 18. Young as they were, I decided not to spend too much money on a person—or garment—who might not be in our lives all that long! I turned to my yarn stash to see what I could put together, and this sweater was the result.

But what happened to Topher? Did he move on and out of our lives? And did we ask for the sweater back? The answer to both questions is "No." He's still very special to my daughter, and I had the original re-knit because it was too cruel to be constantly borrowing it back.

DIFFICULTY — Intermediate

SIZES — Child S (M, L, XL) to fit 2 (4-6, 8, 10-12).
Adult [S, M, L, XL].
Shown in adult size M.

FINISHED MEASUREMENTS — Chest 25½ (30, 34, 38) [42, 46, 50½, 55]"
Length 14½ (16, 19, 22)" [23¾, 25½, 27½, 27½]"

GAUGE — 19 sts and 34 rows to 4"/10cm in Tweed st squares pat using larger needles.

MATERIALS
Main color (MC) in DK weight yarn: 340 (420, 560, 700) [840, 920, 1060, 1200] yds or approx 3 (3, 4, 5) [6, 7, 8, 9] 1¾oz/50g balls in charcoal gray.
Contrast colors (CC) in DK to Aran weight yarn: 2 yd lengths of various yarns in medium to dark intensity reds, red-oranges, oranges, yellow-oranges, yellows, yellow-greens, greens, blue-greens, and blue-purples.
A. Sizes 4 and 6 (3.5 and 4mm) needles, *or size to obtain gauge.*

TWEED ST SQUARES
(Multiple of 10 sts plus 2 selvage sts)
Row 1 With MC, k1 (selvage), *k1, sl 1 purlwise with yarn in front (wyif); rep from* to last st, k1 (selvage).
Row 2 With MC, purl. **Row 3** With CC, k1, *[sl 1 purlwise wyif, k1] 5 times, change CC, rep from* across to last st, k1. **Row 4** With CC, p1, *p10 CC, change to next CC (twisting yarns to avoid holes) and rep from* across to last st, p1. Rep last 4 rows 3 times more (16 rows total

in pat st). Using large photo on p. 74 as guide, change CCs every 16 rows in random color arrangement. Rep these 16 rows for Tweed st squares pat.

Note Child sizes are given first. Adult sizes follow in brackets. If there is only one figure or set of instructions, it applies to all sizes.

BACK
With smaller needles and MC, cast on 62 (70, 82, 90) [102, 110, 122, 130] sts. Work 1 (1, 2, 3) [3]" in k2, p2 rib, end each RS row with k2 and beg each WS row with p2. Change to larger needles. **Next row** (WS) P across and inc 0 (2, 0, 2) [0, 2, 0, 2] sts—62 (72, 82, 92) [102, 112, 122, 132] sts. Work 104 (120, 136, 152) [168, 184, 200, 200] rows in Tweed st squares pat, or 8 rows short of 7 (8, 9, 10) [11, 12, 13, 13] complete squares, end with WS row of CC. Piece measures approx 13½ (15, 18, 21) [22¾, 24½, 26½, 26½]" from beg.
Shape neck
Cont pat, work 20 (24, 28, 32) [36, 41, 45, 50] sts, place next 22 (24, 26, 28) [30, 30, 32, 32] sts on hold, join 2nd length of MC and work to end. Working both sides at same time, work 7 rows more in pat to complete square, AT SAME TIME, bind off 1 st at each neck edge 3 times. Bind off rem 17 (21, 25, 29) [33, 38, 42, 47] sts each side.

FRONT
Work as for back until piece measures approx 12 (13½, 16½, 19½) [20¾, 22½, 24½, 24½]" from beg, or 22 [26] rows less than back, end with WS row of MC.

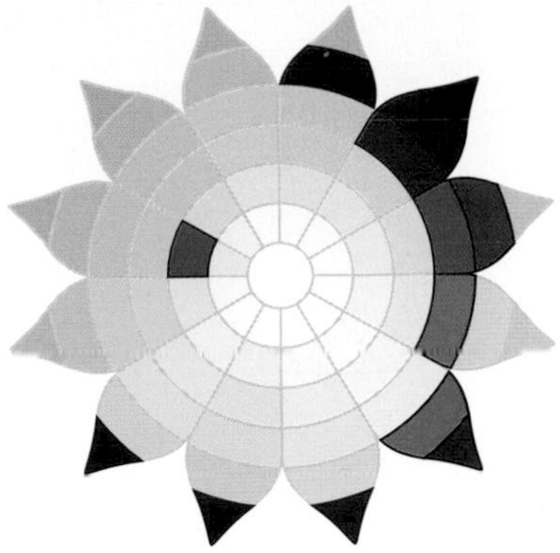

The Color Principles

- MC is darker than CCs; for this garment, MC is dark gray with flecks of reds, oranges, and dark yellows.
- CCs are medium to dark intensity, covering a little more than the warm side of the color wheel (from red to blue-green) with the inclusion of a complementary color (blue-purple).

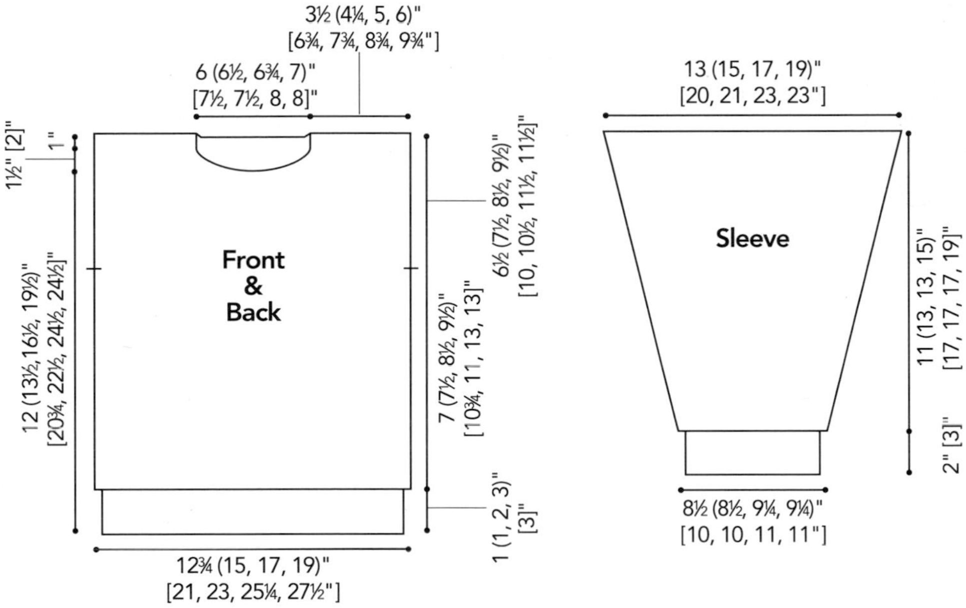

3½ (4¼, 5, 6)"
[6¾, 7¾, 8¾, 9¾"]
6 (6½, 6¾, 7)"
[7½, 7½, 8, 8]"
1½" [2"]
1"
12 (13½,16½, 19½)"
[20¾, 22½, 24½, 24½]"
Front & Back
7 (7½, 8½, 9½)"
[10¾, 11, 13, 13]"
6½ (7½, 8½, 9½)"
[10, 10½, 11½, 11½]"
1 (1, 2, 3)"
[3]"
12¾ (15, 17, 19)"
[21, 23, 25¼, 27½"]
13 (15, 17, 19)"
[20, 21, 23, 23"]
Sleeve
11 (13, 13, 15)"
[17, 17, 17, 19]"
2" [3]"
8½ (8½, 9¼, 9¼)"
[10, 10, 11, 11"]

Shape neck

Cont pat, work 24 (29, 33, 38) [42, 47, 52, 57] sts, place next 14 (14, 16, 16) [18] sts on hold, re-join CC and work to end. Working both sides at same time, bind off from each neck edge 0 (2, 2, 2) [0, 0, 2, 2] sts once, 1 st 7 (6, 6, 7) [9, 9, 8, 8] times—17 (21, 25, 29) [33, 38, 42, 47] sts each side. Work even until piece measures same as back to shoulder. Bind off all sts.

SLEEVES

With smaller needles and MC, cast on 34 (34, 38, 42) [46, 46, 50, 50] sts. Work 2 [3]" in k2, p2 rib as for back. Change to larger needles. **Next row** (WS) P 1 row and inc 8 (8, 4, 0) [6, 6, 2, 2] sts evenly across—42 [52] sts. Work in Tweed st squares pat, AT SAME TIME, inc 1 st each side (working incs inside selvage sts and into pat) every 4th row 0 (0, 10, 16) [0, 7, 24, 15] times, every 6th row 0 (10, 10, 9) [23, 18, 6, 15] times, every 8th row 10 (5, 0, 0) [0] times—62 (72, 82, 92) [98, 102, 112, 112] sts. Work even until piece measures 13 (15, 15, 17) [20, 20, 20, 22]" from beg—approx 6 (7, 7, 8) [9, 9, 9, 10) complete squares. Bind off all sts.

FINISHING

Block pieces. Sew left shoulder.

Neckband

With RS facing, smaller needles, and MC, beg at back neck and pick up and k90 (94, 98, 102) [106, 106, 110, 110] sts around neck edge. Work 1" in k2, p2 rib. Bind off all sts. Sew right shoulder, including neckband.

Place markers 6½, (7½, 8½, 9½) [10, 10½, 11½, 11½]" down from shoulders on front and back. Sew top of sleeves between markers. Sew side and sleeve seams.

TECHNIQUE NOTES

1. It is important that the slip 1 purlwise bars are offset, otherwise the tension will be spoiled. In other words, all the MC slip 1 purlwise bars will line up vertically and all the CC slip 1 purlwise bars will line up on the alternate vertical. Careful attention to the stitch pattern will ensure this.
2. Twist yarns at CC changes to avoid holes.

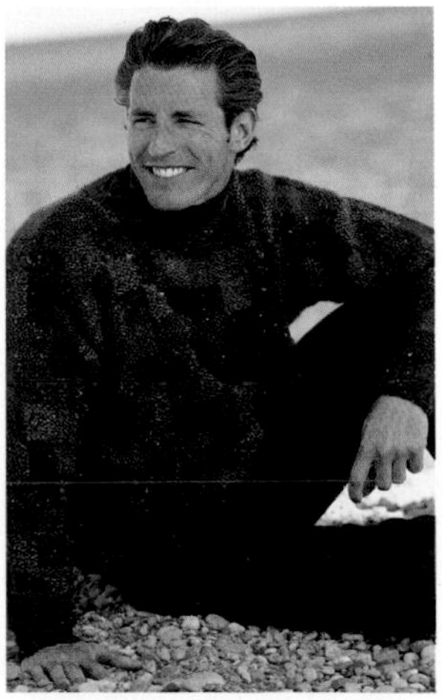

Topher's Pullover
worsted weight version

Students in my Using Up Leftovers workshops have reported that they found this stitch pattern "addictive!" To address this, I offer a number of Tweed stitch squares garments—to deal with the different styles we wear, yarn weights we collect, knitting skills we've mastered, people for whom we knit, and colorways to explore. This pullover is similar to the previous one but in a different yarn weight and colorway.

DIFFICULTY — Intermediate

SIZES — Child S (M, L, XL) to fit sizes 2-4 (6, 8-10, 12-14) Adult [S, M, L] Shown in child's size M

FINISHED MEASUREMENTS — Chest 26½ (31, 35½, 40)" [44½, 49, 53½]" Length 15 (17, 19, 23)" [25, 27, 27]"

GAUGE — 18 sts and 32 rows to 4"/10cm in Tweed st squares pat using larger needles.

MATERIALS

Main color (MC) in worsted weight yarn: 230 (320, 460, 560) [750, 780, 910] yds or approx 2 (3, 4, 5) [7, 7, 8] 1¾oz/50g balls in medium intensity gray.
Contrast colors (CC) in various DK to Aran weight yarns: 2 yd lengths in light intensity yellow-oranges, yellows, yellow-greens, greens, blue-greens, beiges, and off-whites.
A. Sizes 5 and 7 (3.75 and 4.5mm) needles, *or size to obtain gauge.*

TWEED ST SQUARES
(Multiple of 10 sts plus 2 selvage sts)
Row 1 With MC, k1 (selvage), *k1, sl 1 purlwise with yarn in front (wyif); rep from* to last st, k1 (selvage).
Row 2 With MC, purl. **Row 3** With CC, k1, *[sl 1 purlwise wyif, k1] 5 times, change CC, rep from* across to last st, k1. **Row 4** With CC, p1, *p10 CC, change to next CC (twisting yarns to avoid holes) and rep from* across to last st, p1. Rep last 4 rows 3 times more (16 rows total in pat st). Using photo on p. 75 as guide, change CCs every 16 rows in random color arrangement. Rep these 16 rows for Tweed st squares pat.

Note Child sizes are given first. Adult sizes follow in brackets. If there is only one figure or set of instructions, it applies to all sizes.

BACK
With smaller needles and MC, cast on 62 (70, 82, 90) [102, 110, 122] sts. Work 1 (1, 1, 3) [3]" in k2, p2 rib, end each RS row with k2 and beg each WS row with p2. Change to larger needles. **Next row** (WS) P across and inc 0 (2, 0, 2) [0, 2, 0] sts—62 (72, 82, 92) [102, 112,

The Color Principles
• MC is darker than most CCs; for this garment, MC is a medium intensity gray.
• CCs are light to medium intensity, covering approximately one third of the color wheel—for this garment, yellow to blue-green plus beiges and off-whites.

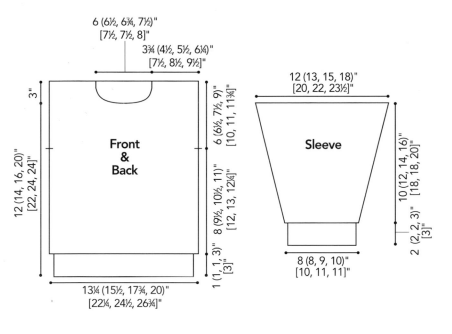

122] sts. Work 112 (128, 144, 160) [176, 192, 192] rows in Tweed st squares pat—7 (8, 9, 10) [11, 12, 12] squares completed and piece measures approx 15 (17, 19, 23) [25, 27, 27]" from beg. Bind off all sts.

FRONT
Work as for back until piece measures 24 rows or 3" less than back, end with a WS row in CC.

Shape neck
Next row (RS) Cont pat, work 25 (30, 34, 39) [44, 49, 54] sts, place 12 (12, 14, 14) [14] sts on hold, join 2nd length of MC and work to end. Working both sides at same time, bind off from each neck edge 2 (3, 3, 2) [2, 2, 3] sts once, 0 (0, 0, 2) [2] sts once, 1 st 6 times. Work even on rem 17 (21, 25, 29) [34, 39, 43] sts each side until piece measures same as back to shoulder. Bind off all sts.

SLEEVES
With smaller needles and MC, cast on 30 (30, 34, 38) [42, 46, 46] sts. Work 2 (2, 2, 3) [3]" in k2, p2 rib as for back. Change to larger needles. **Next row** (WS) P across and inc (8) [4, 6, 6]—38 (38, 42, 46) [46, 52, 52] sts. Work Tweed st squares pat and shape piece simultane-

ously as foll: Work rows 1–2 of pat. **Row 3** (RS) Work selvage st, work pat over 8 (8, 0, 2) [2, 0, 0] sts, work 10-st rep across to last 9 (9, 1, 3) [3, 1, 1] sts, work pat over 8 (8, 0, 2) [2, 0, 0] sts, work selvage st. Cont in pat as established, AT SAME TIME, inc 1 st each side (working incs inside selvage sts and into pat) every 4th row 0 [0, 7, 10] times, every 6th row 0 (0, 4, 12) [23, 18, 18] times, every 8th row 9 (11, 10, 6) [0] times—56 (60, 70, 82) [92, 102, 108] sts. Work even until piece measures approx 12 (14, 16, 19) [21, 21, 23]" from beg—approx 5 (6, 7, 8) [9, 9, 10] complete squares. Bind off all sts.

FINISHING
Block pieces. Sew left shoulder seam.

Neckband
With RS facing, smaller needles, and MC, beg at back neck and pick up and k86 (90, 94, 98) [98, 98, 102] sts evenly around neck edge, including sts on hold. Work 1" in k2, p2 rib. Bind off all sts in rib. Sew right shoulder, including neckband. Place markers 6 (6½, 7½, 9) [10, 11, 11¾]" down from shoulders on front and back. Sew top of sleeves between markers. Sew side and sleeve seams.

TECHNIQUE NOTES
1. It is important that the slip 1 purlwise bars are offset, otherwise the tension will be spoiled. In other words, all the MC slip 1 purlwise bars will line up vertically and all the CC slip 1 purlwise bars will line up on an alternate vertical. Careful attention to the stitch pattern will ensure this.
2. Twist yarns at color changes to avoid holes.

The Whistler Vest

Five years ago, my friends and I met to plan our first ski trip to Whistler, BC. I was then deeply into my addiction to Tweed stitch squares, so I developed this simple vest as a knitting project for the trip. Later, there was some discussion as to how simple it was. Instead of a "beginner slope," one friend described it as "an expert run with moguls." I still think it's pretty simple, but new knitters may need guidance. We all finished our vests, although the new knitter took three years! However, we didn't lose her. She's begun another project!

DIFFICULTY	Beginner knitters with some guidance
SIZES	S (M, L, XL). Shown in size M.
FINISHED MEASUREMENTS	Bust 38 (42, 46, 50)" Length (including crocheted edge) 20 (21½, 21½, 23½)"
GAUGE	19 sts and 34 rows to 4"/10cm using size 6 (4mm) needles in Tweed st squares pat.

MATERIALS

Main color (MC) in DK weight yarn: 360 (440, 500, 580) yds or approx 3 (4, 4, 5) 1¾oz/50g balls in navy.
Contrast colors (CC) in various DK to Aran weight yarns: 2 yd lengths in medium-dark to dark intensity purples, blue-purples, blue-greens, greens, yellow-greens, and browns.
A. Size 6 (4mm) needles, *or size to obtain gauge.*
B. Size E/4 (3.5mm) crochet hook.
C. Five ¾" buttons in CC.

TWEED ST SQUARES

(Multiple of 10 plus 2 selvage sts)
Row 1 With MC, k1 (selvage), *k1, sl 1 purlwise with yarn in front (wyif); rep from* to last st, k1 (selvage). **Row 2** With MC, purl. **Row 3** With CC, k1, *[sl 1 purlwise wyif, k1] 5 times, change CC, rep from* across to last st, k1. **Row 4** With CC, p1, *p10 CC, change to next CC (twisting yarns to avoid holes) and rep from* across to last st, p1. Rep last 4 rows 3 times more (16 rows total in pat st). Using photo on p. 80 as guide, change CCs every 16 rows in random color arrangement. Rep these 16 rows for Tweed st squares pat.

To work half square over 6 sts On row 3, work [sl 1 purlwise wyif, k1] 3 times instead of 5. On row 4, p6 CC.

BACK

With MC, cast on 92 (102, 112, 122) sts. Work 80 (96, 96, 112) rows in Tweed stitch squares pat—5 (6, 6, 7) complete CC squares from beg, end with pat row 16. Piece measures approx 9½ (11, 11, 13)" from beg.
Shape armhole
Cont pat, bind off 10 sts at beg of next 2 rows—72 (82, 92, 102) sts. Working first and last sts as selvage, work 78 rows more in pat—5 full squares from armhole bind-offs. Armhole measures approx 9½". With MC, bind off all sts.

RIGHT FRONT

With MC, cast on 48 (52, 58, 62) sts. Work as for back (**for sizes S and L only,** beg with 1 selvage st, work half square over 6 sts, then work 10-st rep across) until piece measures same as back to armhole, end with pat row 1.
Shape armhole
Pat row 2 (WS) Bind off 10 sts, p to end—38 (42, 48, 52) sts. Work even until 3 full squares have been completed from armhole bind-off, end with pat row 16. Armhole measures approx 5½".
Shape neck
Pat row 1 (RS) Bind off 16 (20, 20, 20) sts, k to end—22 (22, 28, 32) sts. Work even until piece measures same as back to armhole and 5 complete squares have been worked. With MC, bind off all sts.

The Color Principles
- MC is darker than CCs; for this garment, MC is navy.
- CCs are medium-dark to dark intensity, covering two thirds of the color wheel (for this garment, yellow-orange to purple).

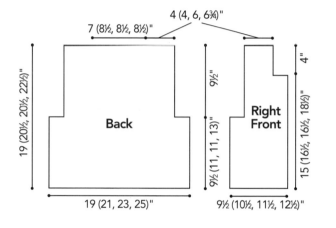

LEFT FRONT

With MC, cast on and work as for right front (for sizes S and L only, work 10-st rep to last 7 sts, work half square over 6 sts, work last st as selvage) until piece measures same as back to armhole, end with pat row 16. Shape armhole by binding off 10 sts at beg of pat row 1, then work even until 3 full squares have been completed from armhole bind-off, end with pat row 15. Shape neck by binding off 16 (20, 20, 20) sts at beg of pat row 16, work to end. Complete as for right front.

FINISHING

Block pieces. Sew shoulder and side seams. With RS facing, work crocheted edgings with MC around armhole and around entire vest as foll:

At armhole

Rnd 1 Beg at underarm, join yarn, ch 2 and work 2 single crochet (sc) for every 3 sts along armhole bind-off, do not work sc in corner, work 2 sc for every 5 rows around armhole, do not work sc in corner, work 2 sc for every 3 sts along armhole bind-off, sl st to beg. Do not turn. **Rnds 2–3** Ch 2, work 1 sc in each sc around, skipping 2 scs at corners and sl st to beg ch-2. Cut yarn and fasten off.

Front and back edgings

Fold back in half and mark midpoint at lower edge. Unless otherwise specified, work 3 sc to turn outside corners, do not work sc at inside corners of neck. **Rnd 1** Beg at marked point, join yarn, ch 2 and work 3 sc for every 4 sts along lower edge to center front, turn corner, 1 sc for every 2 rows along right front to neck, turn corner, 3 sc for every 4 sts along right neck, 1 sc for every 2 rows along right neck to shoulder, 3 sc for every 4 sts along back neck, 1 sc for every 2 rows along left neck, 3 sc for every 4 sts along left neck to corner, turn corner, 1 sc for every 2 rows along left front to corner, turn corner, 3 sc for every 4 sts along lower edge to center back, sl st to beg ch-2. **Rnds 2–3** In same way as armhole, work 2 rnds more in sc, working 3 sts at outside corners of front edges and skipping 2 sc at inside corners of neck, end at center back. Cut yarn. Fasten off.

Buttonband

Join MC to top of left neck edge and work 1 sc in every sc along center front. Cut yarn. Rep from twice more— 3 rows of sc. Sew 5 buttons to band, the first and last approx 1" from neck and lower edge and 3 others spaced evenly between.

Buttonhole band

Join MC to lower edge of right front and work 3 rows in sc as for button band, working buttonholes on first row opposite each button as foll: ch 2, skip 2 sc. On next row, work 2 sc in each ch-2 space.

TECHNIQUE NOTES

1. It is important that the slip 1 purlwise bars are offset, otherwise the tension will be spoiled. In other words, all the MC slip 1 purlwise bars will line up vertically and all the CC slip 1 purlwise bars will line up on an alternate vertical. Careful attention to the stitch pattern will ensure this.
2. Twist yarns at color changes to avoid holes.

Kenneth's Classic Vest

My husband, Ken, taught me to like vests. He asked that every garment I knit for him during our first ten years together be a vest. I have learned to appreciate their versatility, and I now have a closet full— at last count, 24— with ten of them in some version of brown! This vest belongs to my best friend, Laurel, and she often wears it under her intarsia jacket. Making garments out of bits of this and that offers the opportunity to make garments that will automatically coordinate!

DIFFICULTY Advanced

SIZES S (M, L, XL). Shown in size M.

FINISHED MEASUREMENTS Chest 41 (44½, 50½, 54½)"
Length 20 (20, 22, 23)" at back

GAUGE 18 sts and 32 rows to 4"/10cm in Tweed st squares pat using larger needles.

MATERIALS

Main color (MC) in worsted weight yarn: 410 (440, 550, 620) yds or approx 4 (4, 5, 6) 1¾oz/50g balls in charcoal gray.

Contrast colors (CC) in DK to Aran weight yarn: 2 yd lengths of various yarns in light-medium to dark intensity reds, red-purples, purples, blue-purples, blues, blue-greens.

A. Sizes 5 and 7 (3.75 and 4.25mm) needles, *or size to obtain gauge.*

B. Six ⅝" buttons in CCs.

TWEED ST SQUARES

(Multiple of 10 plus 2 selvage sts)

Row 1 With MC, k1 (selvage), *k1, sl 1 purlwise with yarn in front (wyif); rep from* to last st, k1 (selvage). **Row 2** With MC, purl. **Row 3** With CC, k1, *[sl 1 purlwise wyif, k1] 5 times, change CC, rep from* across to last st, k1. **Row 4** With CC, p1, *p10 CC, change to next CC (twisting yarns to avoid holes) and rep from* across to last st, p1. Rep last 4 rows 3 times more (16 rows total in pat st). Using photo on p. 81 as guide, change CCs every 16 rows in random color arrangement. Rep these 16 rows for Tweed st squares pat.

To work half square over 6 sts On row 3, work [sl 1 purlwise wyif, k1] 3 times instead of 5. On row 4, p6 CC.

BACK

With smaller needles and MC, cast on 90 (102, 110, 122) sts. Work 1" in k2, p2 rib, end each RS row with k2 and beg each WS row with p2. Change to larger needles. **Next row** (WS) P across and inc 2 (0, 2, 0) sts—92 (102, 112, 122) sts. Beg with row 9 (9, 1, 9) of Tweed st squares pat, work 72 (72, 80, 88) rows in pat—4½ (4½, 5, 5½) squares and piece measures approx 10 (10, 11, 12)" from beg, end with a WS row.

Shape armhole

Cont pat, bind off 10 sts at beg of next 2 rows—72 (82, 92, 102) sts. Dec 1 st each side every other row 4 (9, 10, 12) times—64 (64, 72, 78) sts. Work even until armhole measures 9 (9, 10, 10)", end with WS row. Mark center 28 sts.

Shape shoulder and neck

Bind off 4 (4, 5, 5) sts at beg of next 2 rows—56 (56, 62, 68) sts. Work both sides separately as foll: **Next row** (RS) *Bind off 4 (4, 5, 6) sts, work to marked center sts, turn. Bind off 1 st (neck), work to end, turn.* Rep between *'s once, then bind off rem sts. Place center 28 sts on hold. With RS facing, join yarn to rem 14 (14, 17, 20) sts, work to end, turn. Working first row as a WS row, rep between *'s twice. Bind off rem sts.

RIGHT FRONT

With smaller needles and MC, cast on 70 (76, 86, 92) sts. **Row 1** (RS) Work 32 (36, 40, 44) sts in k2, p2 rib, k2 (1, 2, 1), place marker (pm), k2 (center sts), pm, k2 (1, 2, 1), work rem 32 (36, 40, 44) sts in p2, k2 rib. **Row 2** P1, inc 1 in next st, work rib as established to 2 sts before marker, work 2 tog, p2 (center sts), work 2

The Color Principles

- MC is darker than the CCs; for this garment, MC is charcoal gray.
- CCs are light-medium to dark intensity, covering one-half of the color wheel—for this garment, the cool side (red to blue-green).

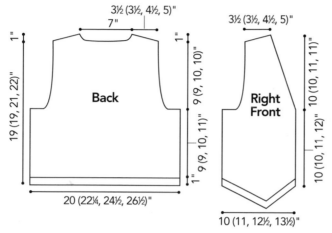

TECHNIQUE NOTES

1. It is important that the slip 1 purlwise bars are offset, otherwise the tension will be spoiled. In other words, all the MC slip 1 purlwise bars will line up vertically and all the CC slip 1 purlwise bars will line up on an alternate vertical. Careful attention to the stitch pattern will ensure this.

2. Twist yarns at color changes to avoid holes.

tog, work rib as established to last 2 sts, inc 1 in next st, p1. Work 5 rows more in rib as established, working row 2 every WS row. Change to larger needles. **Next row (WS)** Rep row 2—70 (76, 86, 92) sts. Cut yarn.

With RS facing, sl sts to right hand needle to 2 center sts. Shape point and dec to 48 (52, 58, 62) as foll: **Beg Right front chart: Row 1** (RS) With CC (MC, MC, CC) work 2 (center) sts; turn. **Row 2** (WS) P2, p2tog, p1; turn. **Row 3**

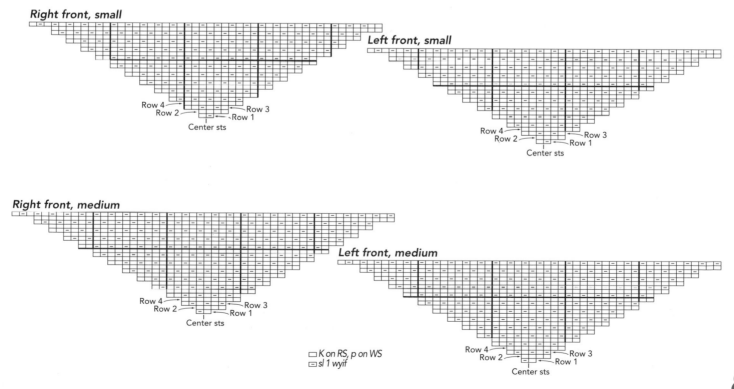

□ K on RS, p on WS
□ sl 1 wyif

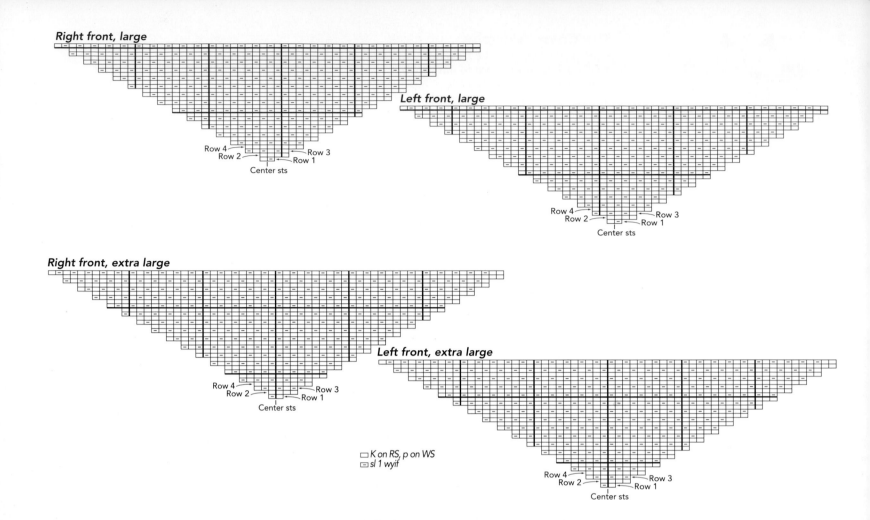

Right front, large

Row 4
Row 2
Row 3
Row 1
Center sts

Left front, large

Row 4
Row 2
Row 3
Row 1
Center sts

Right front, extra large

Row 4
Row 2
Row 3
Row 1
Center sts

Left front, extra large

☐ K on RS, p on WS
☐ sl 1 wyif

Row 4
Row 2
Row 3
Row 1
Center sts

Work to break between sts of garment piece and rib, k2tog, work 1 st; turn. **Row 4** Work to break, p2tog, p1; turn. Rep rows 3–4 and work through chart as established until 4 (4, 0, 0) sts rem from rib at each end, end with RS row. **For sizes S, M only** (WS) Work to break, p2tog, p2; turn, work to break, work k2tog, work 2. Cont in pat as established (**for size S, L only** work half squares at center front) until piece measures same as back to armhole, end with WS row.

Shape neck and armhole

Next row (RS) Dec 1 st (neck edge), work to end. **Next row** (WS) Bind off 10 sts, work to end—37 (41, 47, 51) sts. Shape armhole as for back, AT SAME TIME, dec 1 st at neck edge every 4th row 17 (16, 17, 16) times more— 16 (16, 20, 23) sts. Work even until armhole measures same as back to shoulder, end with RS row.

Shape shoulder

At shoulder edge, bind off 4 (4, 5, 5) sts once, 4 (4, 5, 6) 3 times.

LEFT FRONT

Work as for right front, working from left front chart and reversing all shaping.

FINISHING

Note Button and buttonhole bands are worked for a man's garment. Reverse bands for woman's garments. Block pieces. Sew shoulder seams. Work all bands with RS facing, smaller needles, and MC.

Buttonband

Beg at lower edge of right front and pick up and k3 sts for every 4 rows to beg of V-neck, work k1, yo, k1 into st at point of V, 5 sts for every 6 rows from V to shoulder seam, 5 sts along back neck shaping, 14 sts from holder. Work 8 rows in k2, p2 rib. Bind off all sts. Sew buttons on band, the first at point of V, the last 1" from lower edge, and 3 others spaced evenly between.

Buttonhole band

Beg at center back and k14 sts from holder, pick up and k5 sts along back neck shaping, 5 sts for every 6 rows from shoulder to point of V, work k1, yo, k1 into st at point of V, 3 sts for every 4 rows to lower edge of left front. Work 8 rows in k2, p2 rib and beg on 3rd row, work 3-row buttonholes (see Appendix, p. 138) opposite buttons. Bind off all sts. Sew bands at center back.

Armhole bands

Beg at underarm and pick up and k1 st for every bound-off st at underarm and 3 sts for every 4 rows around armhole. Work 8 rows in k2, p2 rib. Bind off all sts. Sew side seams, including armbands.

Ski Suit Cardigan

Immediately after finishing the original Topher's pullover, I wanted to make something for myself in the same color range but a different style. So, I took some dark gold wool I had bought at a fair and the same CCs used in Topher's pullover to make this sweater. I made it very short so it would work under my one piece ski suit. The sleeves are 3" longer than necessary so I can pull them into my ski mitts. You may, of course, make the sleeves shorter and the body longer.

DIFFICULTY	Intermediate
SIZES	S (M, L). Shown in size S.
FINISHED MEASUREMENTS	Bust 41½ (45¼, 50½)" Length 17½ (19, 20½)"
GAUGE	18 sts and 32 rows to 4"/10cm in Tweed st squares pat. And 20 sts and 27 rows to 4"/10cm in k2, p2 rib, well blocked, using larger needles.

MATERIALS

Main color (MC) in worsted weight yarn: 620 (750, 900) yds or approx 6 (7, 8) 1¾oz/50g balls in dark intensity yellow-orange.

Contrast colors (CC) in various DK to Aran weight yarns: 2 yd lengths of medium to dark intensity red, orange-red, orange, yellow-orange, yellow, yellow-green, green, blue-green, and blue-purple.

A. Sizes 5 and 7 (3.75 and 4.5mm) needles, *or size to obtain gauge*.

B. Five ¾" buttons in MC.

TWEED ST SQUARES

(Multiple of 10 plus 2 selvage sts)

Row 1 With MC, k1 (selvage), *k1, sl 1 purlwise with yarn in front (wyif); rep from* to last st, k1 (selvage). **Row 2** With MC, purl. **Row 3** With CC, k1, *[sl 1 purlwise wyif, k1] 5 times, change CC, rep from* across to last st, k1. **Row 4** With CC, p1, *p10 CC, change to next CC (twisting yarns to avoid holes) and rep from* across to last st, p1. Rep last 4 rows 3 times more (16 rows total in pat st). Using photo on p. 85 as guide, change CCs every 16 rows in random color arrangement. Rep these 16 rows for Tweed st squares pat.

To work half square over 6 sts On row 3, work [sl 1 purlwise wyif, k1] 3 times instead of 5. On row 4, p6 CC.

BACK

With smaller needles and MC, cast on 90 (102, 110) sts. Work 1" in k2, p2 rib, end each RS row with k2 and beg each WS row with p2. Change to larger needles. **Next row** (WS) P 1 row and inc 2 (0, 2) sts evenly across—92 (102, 112) sts. Work 64 (72, 80) rows in Tweed st squares pat—4 (4½, 5) complete squares and piece measures approx 9 (10, 11)" from beg, end with WS row 16 (8, 16).

Shape armhole

Cont pat, bind off 5 sts at beg of next 2 rows—82 (92, 102) sts. Dec 1 st each side every other row 5 (7, 9) times—72 (78, 84) sts. Work even until armhole measures 7½ (8, 8½)", end with a WS row.

Shape shoulders

Bind off 4 (5, 6) sts at beg of next 4 rows, 5 (5, 6) sts at beg of next 2 rows, 5 (6, 6) sts at beg of next 2 rows. Place rem 36 sts on hold.

RIGHT FRONT

With smaller needles and MC, cast on 46 (50, 58) sts. Work 1" in k2, p2 rib as for back. Change to larger needles. **Next row** (WS) P 1 row and inc 2 (2, 0) sts evenly across—48 (52, 58) sts. Work in Tweed st squares pat (**for sizes S and L only**, beg with 1 selvage st, work half square over 6 sts, then work 10-st rep across). When piece measures same as back to armhole, end with a RS row.

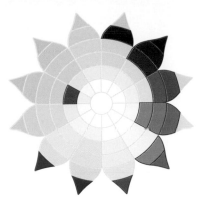

The Color Principles
- MC is dark intensity; for this garment, MC is dark yellow-orange.
- CCs are medium to dark intensity, covering a little more than the warm side of the color wheel (from red to blue-green) with the inclusion of a complementary color (blue-purple).
- The bright yellow-orange CC is a little intense for the rest of the colors, but I wanted to use it because it echoes the color of the stitching on my ski suit. However, its use here does illustrate the principle "Once is a mistake, twice is a problem, and three times is a design."(Thanks to Lee Andersen of Columbia, Maryland for this expression!) Seems I should have used it more often or not at all!

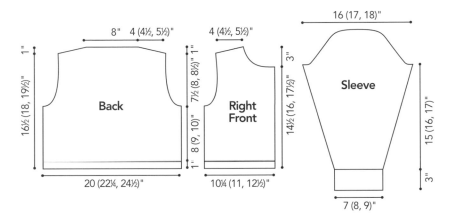

Shape armhole
Next row (WS) Cont pat, bind off 5 sts, work to end—43 (47, 53) sts. Dec 1 st at armhole every other row 5 (7, 9) times—38 (40, 44) sts. Work even until armhole measures 5½ (6, 6½)", end with WS row.

Shape neck
Next row (RS) Bind off 10 sts, work to end. At neck edge, bind off 3 sts once, 2 sts once, 1 st 5 (4, 5) times—18 (21, 24) sts. Work even until armhole measures same as back to shoulder, end with a RS row.

Shape shoulder
At shoulder edge, bind off 4 (5, 6) sts twice, 5 (5, 6) sts once, 5 (6, 6) sts once. Bind off rem sts.

LEFT FRONT
Cast on, work rib and inc as for right front. **For sizes S, L only**, work 10-st rep to last 7 sts, work half square over 6 sts, work last st as selvage. Complete as for right front, reversing all shaping.

SLEEVES
With smaller needles and MC, cast on 38 (42, 46) sts. Work 3" in k2, p2 rib as for back. Change to larger needles. Cont in rib, AT SAME TIME, inc 1 st each side (working incs after first 2 and before last 2 sts and working them into rib pat) every 4th row 23 (19, 17) times, every 6th row 0 (4, 6) times—84 (88, 92) sts. Work even until piece measures 18 (19, 20)" from beg, end with a WS row.

Shape cap
Bind off 6 sts at beg of next 2 rows—72 (76, 80) sts.
Next (dec) row (RS) K2, ssk, rib to last 4 sts, k2tog, k2. Work 1 row even. Rep last 2 rows 17 (19, 21) times more—36 sts. Bind off 2 sts at beg of next 2 rows, 4 sts at beg of next 2 rows, 6 sts at beg of next 2 rows. Bind off rem sts.

FINISHING
Block pieces. Sew shoulder seams. Work all bands with RS facing, smaller needles and MC.

Neckband
Beg at right front neck and pick up and k90 sts evenly around neck edge. Work 1" in k2, p2 rib. Bind off all sts.

Buttonband
Beg at top of left neckband and pick up and k3 sts for every 4 rows to lower edge. Work 6 rows in k2, p2 rib. Bind off all sts. Sew 5 buttons to band, the first at neckband, the last in rib at lower edge, and 3 others spaced evenly between.

Buttonhole band
Beg at lower edge of right front and pick up and k3 sts for every 4 rows to top of neckband. Work as for buttonband, working 3-row buttonholes opposite buttons beg in row 3. Bind off all sts.
Set in sleeves. Sew side and sleeve seams.

TECHNIQUE NOTES
1. It is important that the slip 1 purlwise bars are offset, otherwise the tension will be spoiled. In other words, all the MC slip 1 purlwise bars will line up vertically and all the CC slip 1 purlwise bars will line up on an alternate vertical. Careful attention to the stitch pattern will ensure this.
2. Twist yarns at color changes to avoid holes.

Tweed stitch with cables

I love to combine stitch

patterns—cables

interspersed with bobbles

against knit and purl

patterns mixed with lace.

This kind of complexity did

not seem to have a place in

a book about combining

yarns and colors.

But I did develop and

include one group of

garments that explore

both yarn and stitch

pattern combinations,

and here they are.

The garments in this section off-set simple cables against tweed stitch squares. In other words, cables begin and end in mid-fabric, centered over the previous area of tweed stitch.

Normally, when we introduce cables in the middle of a fabric, we get puckers. The fabric above and below the cables will bulge because the cables pull stitches together to a tighter gauge. To avoid this, allowances are made for this altered gauge.

In the stitch pattern for these garments, there are 4-stitch cables flanked by single purl stitches. To avoid puckering, the cables begin not over 6 stitches (p1, k4, p1) but over 4 sts (p1, k2, p1). The 2 knit stitches are increased to 4 just before the first cable twist and then decreased to 2 after the last cable twist. In this way, the cable has the stitches it needs, and the fabric above and below the cable is not distorted.

Because of the work done to accommodate the cables against the tweed stitch, I imagined the garments of this section as more complex pieces. And they are. The two women's garments—the Dress-up Vest and Annalee's Jacket—have side shaping, and it requires the skills of an advanced knitter to work this shaping through the alternating stitch patterns.

At the same time, you might notice that the garments in this section are all worked in extremely limited colors. In the women's garments, off-whites and creams, light and dark taupes, and charcoal grays are all the colors you will see. Why? It seemed to me that with all the complexity of "noise" going on in the stitch patterns, perhaps the colors should remain fairly quiet. Also, I liked the challenge of making dressy, elegant garments out of bits of this and that. But most significantly, we all have a favorite color, so why not offer garments worked in a single color?

Speaking of a single color, check out Randy's Pullover. It's shown in green, but who in the world has so many subtle variations of green in a stash? Not me! This garment was produced by knitting together a riot of colors (see "before" garment on p. 18) and then overdyeing. The process was fun, and the result is gorgeous!

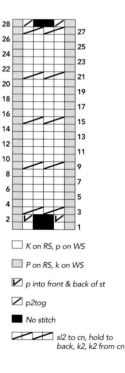

☐ K on RS, p on WS

☐ P on RS, k on WS

◩ p into front & back of st

◪ p2tog

■ No stitch

▧ sl2 to cn, hold to back, k2, k2 from cn

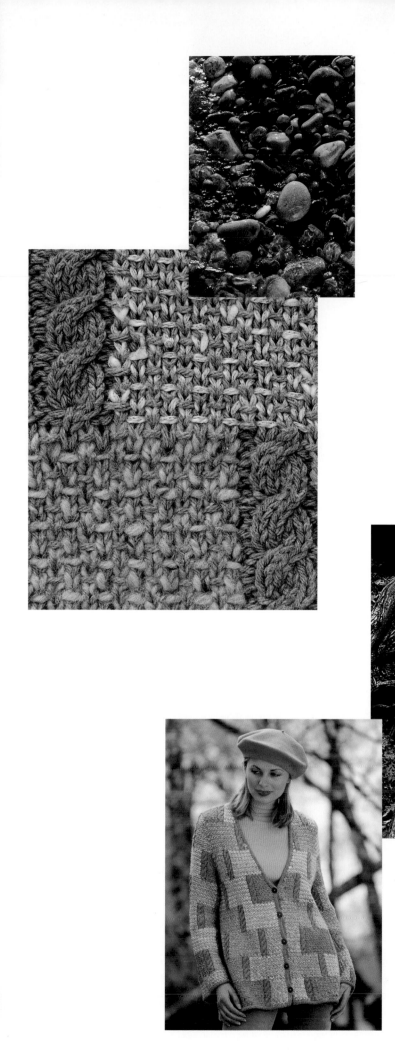

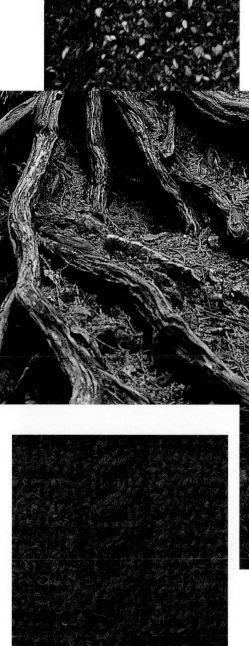

ACCEPTING
CHALLENGES
It's fine to rely on
stitch patterns you
love. But we all
need challenges
to keep us learning
and moving
forward. So, try
altering these
favorites to create
something new. And
once in a
while, I highly
recommend doing
a piece of knitting
that is totally
uncharacteristic
for you.

Randy's Pullover

This garment was made to be overdyed, so I first worked it in a quite horrible range of colors. The "before" garment is shown on page 18, and the dyeing "recipe" is given in The Color Principles. Many men I know seem to prefer subtle color changes, so this technique is perfect for them. Randy is my step-son-in-law—husband to Annalee and father to my grandchildren—and I made this garment with him in mind. I showed him the "before" because he understands overdyeing and has a strong heart. But it also made him appreciate the "after!"

DIFFICULTY	Intermediate
SIZES	S (M, L, XL). Shown in size M.
FINISHED MEASUREMENTS	Chest 44 (47, 50, 53)" Length 25 (27, 28, 29)"
GAUGE	21 sts and 37 rows to 4"/10cm in Tweed st pat using larger size needles.

MATERIALS

Note Garment was overdyed. See The Color Principles.
Main color (MC) In DK weight yarn: 1200 (1300, 1460, 1640) yds or approx 9 (10, 11, 12) 1¾oz/50g balls in medium-dark color; 2 yd lengths of same yarn are used for cables.
Contrast colors (CC) 4½ yd lengths of DK to worsted weight yarns in various colors.
A. Sizes 4 and 6 (3.5 and 4mm) needles, *or size to obtain gauge.*
B. Cable needle (cn).

STITCH PATTERNS

Tweed stitch (over a multiple of 2 sts)
Row 1 (RS) With CC, *sl 1 purlwise with yarn in front (wyif), k1; rep from*. **Row 2** With CC, purl. **Row 3** With MC, *k1, sl 1 purlwise wyif; rep from*. **Row 4** With MC, purl. Rep rows 1–4 for Tweed st pat, changing CCs every 28 rows.
Cable pat (over 4 sts inc'd to 6 sts, then dec'd to 4 sts)
Row 1 (RS) P1, k2, p1. **Row 2** K1, [p into front and back of next st] twice, k1—6 sts. **Row 3** P1, sl 2 to cn and hold to back of work, k2; k2 from cn, p1. **Rows 4–8**

K the knit sts and p the purl sts. **Rows 9–26** Rep rows 3–8 a total of 3 times. **Row 27** Rep row 3. **Row 28** K1, [p2tog] twice, k1—4 sts. Rep rows 1–28 for cable pat.

Note Every 28 rows, Tweed st and Cable pats are offset with a new cable positioned over center 4 sts of previous Tweed st section.

BACK

With smaller needles and MC, cast on 118 (126, 134, 142) sts. Work 3" in k2, p2 rib, end each RS row with k2 and beg each WS row with p2. Change to larger needles. P 1 row.
Establish pats as foll: Beg and end with 4½ (0, 1, 2) yd lengths of CC for first and last Tweed st pats. Use 4½ yd lengths for all other CCs and 2 yd lengths of MC to work Cable pat. Beg with row 1 of Tweed st and Cable pats.
Beg pats: Row 1 (RS) K1 CC (MC, CC, CC) (selvage), work 16 (0, 4, 8) sts Tweed st in CC, [4 sts Cable in MC, 16 sts Tweed st in CC] 5 (6, 6, 6) times, **for size S,** end k1 CC (selvage), **for sizes M, L, XL,** work 4 sts Cable in MC, 0 (4, 8) sts Tweed st in CC, k1 MC (CC, CC) (selvage). **Row 2** (WS) P first and last st in CC (MC, CC, CC) and work rem sts in Tweed and Cable pats as established. Work 26 more pat rows.
Alternate pats as foll: Change CCs. Beg and end with 2 (3, 4, 5) yd lengths of CC for first and last Tweed st pats. Use 4½ yd lengths for all other CCs and 2 yd lengths of MC to work Cable pat. **Row 1** (RS) K1 CC, work 6 (10, 14, 18) sts Tweed st in CC, [4 sts Cable in MC, 16 sts Tweed st in CC] 5 times, work 4 sts Cable in MC, 6 (10,

The Color Principles
- Garment was overdyed (see Try overdyeing, p. 17) with Dylon: 3 packages of medium gray, and 1 package each in deep blue, olive green, tobacco brown, and dark brown resulting in a dark intensity yellow-green.
- There's no need to match original MC and CC, but we list them here for your interest.
- MC was medium-dark intensity; for this garment, green, with 3 different yarns used for ribbings, MC in body and in sleeves.
- CCs were lighter colors; colors before dyeing are shown on color wheel.
- All yarns were 100% wool; garment could also be done in 100% cotton yarns.

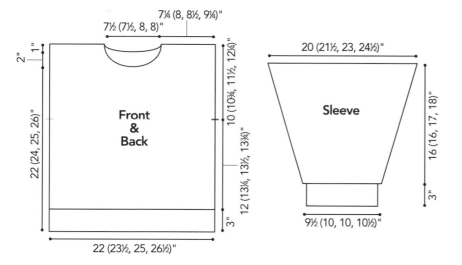

14, 18) sts Tweed st in CC, k1 CC. Work 27 more pat rows as established. Rep last 56 rows for pat, changing CCs every 28 rows. Work even until piece measures 24 (26, 27, 28)" from beg, end with a WS row.

Shape neck
Next row (RS) Cont pat, work 41 (45, 48, 52) sts, place next 36 (36, 38, 38) sts on hold, join 2nd lengths of yarn, work to end. Working both sides at same time, bind off 1 st from each neck edge twice. Bind off rem 39 (43, 46, 50) sts each side.

FRONT
Work as for back until piece measures 22 (24, 25, 26)" from beg, end with a WS row.

Shape neck
Next row (RS) Cont pat, work 49 (53, 57, 61) sts, place next 20 sts on hold, join 2nd lengths of yarn and work to end. Working both sides at same time, bind off from each neck edge 2 sts 1 (1, 2, 2) times, 1 st 8 (8, 7, 7) times. Work even until piece measures same as back to shoulder. Bind off all sts.

SLEEVES
With smaller needles and MC, cast on 46 (46, 50, 50) sts. Work 3" in k2, p2 rib as for back. Change to larger needles.

P 1 row and inc 4 (8, 4, 8) sts evenly across—50 (54, 54, 58) sts. **Establish pats** Beg and end with 1 (1½, 1½, 2) yd lengths of CC for first and last Tweed st pats. Use 4½ yd lengths for all other CCs and 2 yd lengths of MC to work Cable pat. **Beg pat: Row 1** (RS) K1 CC (selvage), work 2 (4, 4, 6) sts Tweed st in CC, [4 sts Cable in MC, 16 sts Tweed st in CC] twice, work 4 sts Cable in MC, 2 (4, 4, 6) sts Tweed st in CC, k1 CC (selvage). Cont in pats as established (changing CCs after 28 rows and staggering Cable and Tweed st pats as on back), AT SAME TIME, inc 1 st each side every 4th row 17 (17, 28, 32) times, every 6th row 12 (12, 6, 4) times—108 (112, 122, 130) sts. Work even until piece measures 19 (19, 20, 21)" from beg. Bind off all sts.

FINISHING
Block pieces. Sew left shoulder.

Neckband
With RS facing, smaller needles, and MC, beg at right back neck and pick up and k114 (114, 118, 118) sts evenly around neck edge. Beg with p2 on WS row, work 1" in k2, p2 rib. Bind off all sts. Sew right shoulder, including neckband. Place markers 10 (10¾, 11½, 12¼)" down from shoulders on front and back. Sew top of sleeves between markers. Sew side and sleeve seams.

TECHNIQUE NOTES
1. Twist yarns at contrast color changes to avoid holes.
2. Two of every four rows are worked across with a ball of MC. Carry MC loosely up side of work.
3. Two of every four rows are worked in CC with MC cables. 2 yd lengths of MC are required to work cables on these CC rows.

Dress-Up Vest

This garment, like the rest in this section, is made in extremely limited colors. The result here is a vest that looks pretty elegant— nice enough for "dress-up". I limited the color changes to balance the changes in yarn and the changes in stitch pattern from tweed to cables. Funny thing though . . . I did not think this through at the time. I just kept knitting garments in quiet neutrals. Sometimes it's fun to let instinct work and let the analysis come later.

DIFFICULTY	Advanced
SIZES	S (M, L, XL). Shown in size M.
FINISHED MEASUREMENTS	Bust 41 (43, 45, 47)" Length 26½ (27½, 28½, 28½)"
GAUGE	18 sts and 33 rows to 4"/10cm in Tweed st pat using larger needles.

MATERIALS

Main color (MC) In DK weight yarn: 560 (600, 660, 700) yds or approx 4 (5, 5, 5) 1¾oz/50g balls in dark brown/charcoal tweed; 2 yd lengths of same yarn is used for cables.
Contrast colors (CC) Lengths of DK to Aran weight yarns in slightly lighter grays, taupes and browns than MC; see table on next page for specific lengths.
A. Sizes 5 and 7 (3.75 and 4.5mm) needles, *or size to obtain gauge.*

B. Cable needle (cn).
C. Seven ⅝" buttons in MC (round neck) or five ⅝" buttons in MC (V-neck).

STITCH PATTERNS
Tweed stitch (multiple of 2 sts)
Row 1 (RS) With CC, *sl 1 purlwise with yarn in front (wyif), k1; rep from*. **Row 2** With CC, purl. **Row 3** With MC, *k1, sl 1 purlwise wyif; rep from*. **Row 4** With MC, purl. Rep rows 1–4 for Tweed st pat, changing CCs every 28 rows.
Cable pat (over 4 sts inc'd to 6 sts, then dec'd to 4 sts)
Row 1 (RS) P1, k2, p1. **Row 2** K1, [p into front and back of next st] twice, k1—6 sts. **Rows 3** P1, sl 2 to cn and hold to back of work, k2; k2 from cn, p1. **Rows 4–8** K the knit sts and p the purl sts. **Rows 9–26** Rep rows 3–8 a total of 3 times more. **Row 27** Rep row 3. **Row 28** K1, [p2tog] twice, k1—4 sts. Rep rows 1–28 for cable pat.

Note Every 28 rows, Tweed st and Cable pats are offset with a new cable positioned over center 4 sts of previous Tweed st section.

BACK
With smaller needles and MC, cast on 114 (118, 122, 126) sts. **Work edging** Work 4 rows rev St st [p on RS, k on WS], end with a WS row. Change to larger needles. **Establish pats as foll:** Use first tier of drawing on next page as guide for pat and st placement. Beg with row 1 of Tweed st and Cable pats. **Beg pats: Row 1** (RS) K1 CC (selvage), work 14 (16, 18, 20) sts Tweed st in CC, *4 sts Cable in MC, 16 sts Tweed st in CC; rep from* to last 19 (21, 23, 25) sts, work 4 sts Cable in MC, 14 (16, 18, 20) sts Tweed st in CC, end k1 CC (selvage). **Row 2** (WS) P first and last st in CC and work rem sts in Tweed and Cable pats as established. Work 26 more pat rows, AT SAME TIME, dec 1 st each side every 12th row twice—110 (114, 118, 122) sts.
Alternate pats as foll: Change CCs. Foll 2nd tier of drawing, work 28 rows more in pat and dec 1 st each side every 12th row twice—106 (110, 114, 118) sts. Change CCs. Foll 3rd tier of drawing, work 28 rows more in pat and dec 1 st each side every 12th row 3 times—100 (104, 108, 112) sts. Cont to alternate pats and change CCs every 28 rows, AT SAME TIME, dec 1 st each side every 12th row 3 times more—94 (98, 102,

The Color Principles
- MC is darker than CCs; for this garment, MC is dark brown/charcoal tweed.
- CCs are in medium-dark to dark intensities—for this garment, grays, taupes, and browns.
- An extremely limited color range is used; if working with more color, stick to perhaps two adjacent colors of the color wheel.

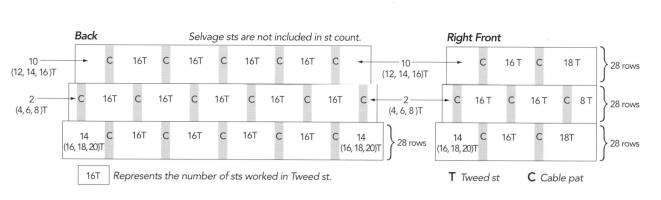

Length of CC required to work 28 rows	sts
1½ yds. –	4 sts
2 yds. –	6 sts
2½ yds. –	8 sts
3 yds. –	10 sts
3½ yds. –	12 sts
4 yds. –	14 sts
4½ yds. –	16 sts
5 yds. –	18 sts
5½ yds. –	20 sts
6 yds. –	22 sts
6½ yds. –	24 sts

Back — Selvage sts are not included in st count.

Right Front

| 16T | Represents the number of sts worked in Tweed st. |

T *Tweed st*   C *Cable pat*

106) sts. Work even in pats as established until piece measures 15½ (16½, 17½, 17½)" from beg, end with a WS row.

Shape armhole
Cont pats, bind off 9 sts at beg of next 2 rows, 2 sts at beg of next 2 rows. Dec 1 st each side every other row 6 (5, 5, 5) times—60 (66, 70, 74) sts. Work even until armhole measures 10", end with a WS row. Mark center 32 sts (round neck) or 24 sts (V-neck).

Round neck version: Shape shoulders and neck
Bind off 3 (3, 4, 4) sts at beg of next 2 rows—54 (60, 62, 66) sts. **Next row** (RS) *Bind off 3 (4, 4, 5) sts, work to marked sts, turn. Bind off 1 st (neck edge), work to end.* Rep between *'s once. Bind off rem sts. Place center 32 sts on hold. With RS facing, join yarn to rem sts, work to end. Rep between *'s twice (binding off shoulder sts at beg of WS row). Bind off rem sts.

V-neck version: Shape shoulder and neck
Bind off 4 (4, 5, 5) sts at beg of next 2 rows—52 (58, 60, 64) sts. **Next row** (RS) *Bind off 4 (5, 5, 6) sts, work to marked sts, turn. Bind off 1 st (neck edge), work to end.* Rep between *'s once. Bind off rem sts. Place center 24 sts on hold. With RS facing, join yarn to rem sts, work to end. Rep between *'s twice (binding off shoulder sts at beg of WS row). Bind off rem sts.

RIGHT FRONT
With smaller needles and MC, cast on 58 (60, 62, 64) sts. Work edging as for back. Change to larger needles.
Establish pats as foll Use first tier of drawing as guide

for pat and st placement. **Beg pats: Row 1** (RS) K1 CC (selvage), work 18 sts Tweed st in CC, 4 sts Cable in MC, 16 sts Tweed st in CC, 4 sts Cable in MC, 14 (16, 18, 20) Tweed st in CC, k1 CC (selvage). **Row 2** (WS) P first and last st in CC and work rem sts in Tweed and Cable pats as established. Work 26 more pat rows, AT SAME TIME, dec 1 st at side edge (end of RS row) every 12th row twice—56 (58, 60, 62) sts.
Alternate pats as foll Change CCs. Foll 2nd tier of drawing, work 28 rows more in pats and dec 1 st at side edge every 12th row twice—54 (56, 58, 60) sts. Change CCs. Foll 3rd tier of drawing, work 28 more rows in pat and cont to dec 1 st at side edge every 12th row 3 times—51 (53, 55, 57) sts. Cont to alternate pats and change CCs each 28 rows while dec 1 st at side edge every 12th row 3 times more—48 (50, 52, 54) sts. Work even in pats as established until piece measures same as back to armhole, end with a RS row.

Round neck version
Shape armhole: Next row (WS) Bind off 9 sts, work to end—39 (41, 43, 45) sts. At armhole, bind off 2 sts once, then dec 1 st at armhole every other row 6 (5, 5, 5) times—31 (34, 36, 38) sts. Work even until armhole measures 8", end with a WS row.
Shape neck and shoulder: Next row (RS) Bind off 10 sts, work to end—21 (24, 26, 28) sts. At neck edge, bind off 3 sts once, 2 sts once, 1 st 4 times—12 (15, 17, 19) sts. Work even until armhole measures same as back to shoulder, end with a RS row. Shape shoulder at beg of WS rows as for back.

TECHNIQUE NOTES
1. Twist yarns at CC changes to avoid holes.
2. Two of every four rows are worked across with a ball of MC. Carry MC loosely up side of work.
3. Two of every four rows are worked in CC with MC cables. 2 yd lengths of MC are required to work cables on these CC rows.
4. Pattern contains options for V and round neck shaping.

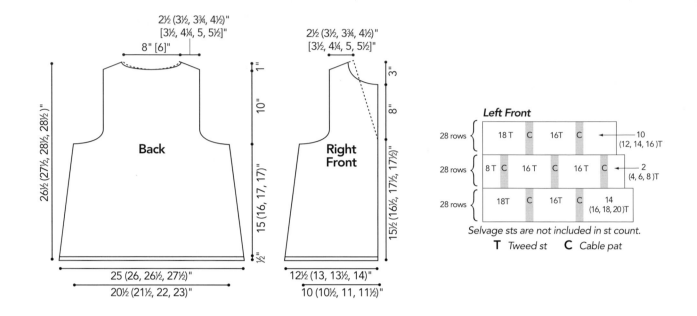

Back

2½ (3½, 3¾, 4½)"
[3½, 4¼, 5, 5½]"
8" [6]"

26½ (27¼, 28¼, 28½)"

1"
10"
15 (16, 17, 17)"
½"

25 (26, 26½, 27½)"
20½ (21½, 22, 23)"

Right Front

2½ (3½, 3¾, 4½)"
[3½, 4¼, 5, 5½]"
3"
8"
15½ (16½, 17½, 17½)"

12½ (13, 13½, 14)"
10 (10½, 11, 11½)"

Left Front

28 rows	18 T	C	16 T	C	← 10 (12, 14, 16)T
28 rows	8 T C 16 T C 16 T C				← 2 (4, 6, 8)T
28 rows	18T C 16T C 14 (16, 18, 20)T				

Selvage sts are not included in st count.
T Tweed st   **C** Cable pat

V-neck version

Shape armhole and V-neck: Next row (WS) Bind off 9 sts, work to end. **Next row** (RS) Dec 1 st (neck edge), work to end—38 (40, 42, 44) sts. At armhole, bind off 2 sts once, then dec 1 st every other row 6 (5, 5, 5) times, AT SAME TIME, dec 1 st at neck edge every 4th row 14 times more. Work even until armhole measures same as back to shoulder, end with a RS row. Shape shoulder at beg of WS rows as for back.

LEFT FRONT

Cast on and work edging as for right front. Change to larger needles.
Establish pats as foll Use first tier of drawing as guide for pat and st placement. **Beg pats: Row 1** (RS) K1 CC (selvage), work 14 (16, 18, 20) sts Tweed st in CC, 4 sts Cable in MC, 16 sts Tweed st in CC, 4 sts Cable in MC, 18 sts Tweed st in CC, k1 CC (selvage). Using left front drawing as guide, work to correspond to right front, dec at side edge and reversing armhole, neck, and shoulder shaping.

FINISHING

Block pieces. Sew shoulder seams. **For both versions,** work all bands as foll: With RS facing, smaller needles, and MC, pick up sts as instructed. Complete rev St st band by working [k 1 row, p 1 row] twice. Bind off all sts.
Round neck version
Neckband Beg at right front neck edge and pick up and k106 sts evenly around neck, including sts on hold. Complete band.

Buttonband Beg at left front neck edge and pick up and k2 sts for every 3 rows to lower edge. Complete band. Sew 7 buttons between band and body, the first 1" from neck edge, the last 6" from lower edge, and 5 others spaced evenly between.
Buttonhole band Beg at lower right front edge and pick up and k2 sts for every 3 rows to neck edge, AT SAME TIME, work buttonholes by casting on 2 sts (instead of picking up 2 sts) opposite each button. Complete band.
V- neck version
Buttonband Beg at center back neck, and k12 sts on hold, pick up and k5 sts along left back neck shaping, 3 sts for every 4 rows to point of V, work k1, yo, k1 into st at point of V, 2 sts for every 3 rows to lower edge. Complete band. Sew 5 buttons between band and body, the first at point of V, the last 6" from lower edge, and 3 others spaced evenly between.
Buttonhole band Beg at lower right front edge and pick up and k2 sts for every 3 rows to point of V, AT SAME TIME, work buttonholes by casting on 1 st (instead of picking up 1 st) opposite each button; then cont to pick up and work k1, yo, k1 into st at point of V, 3 sts for every 4 rows from V to shoulder, 5 sts along back neck shaping, k12 sts on hold. Complete band. Sew bands tog at back neck.
For both versions
Armbands Beg at underarm and pick up and k1 st for every bound-off st at underarm and 3 sts for every 4 rows around armhole edge. Complete band.
Sew side seams, including armbands.

Annalee's Jacket

The limited color range of this garment gives it the same classy, elegant, dressy look of the previous one. It's perfect for my stepdaughter Annalee who works in a large Canadian insurance company. Somehow, when we think of using up our leftovers, it presupposes using up lots of yarn in lots of colors, but the latter is not necessary. We all have favorite colors that we have lots of in our stash or that we gravitate towards in a yarn shop. These garments, I hope, illustrate that you can make wonderful fabrics without moving far from these favorite colors. Any of the garments in this book could be made this way.

DIFFICULTY Advanced

SIZES S (M, L, XL). Shown in size M.

FINISHED Bust 41 (43, 45, 47)"
MEASUREMENTS Length 26 (27½, 29, 29½)"

GAUGE 18 sts and 33 rows to 4"/10cm in Tweed st pat, using larger needles.

MATERIALS

Main color (MC) In DK weight yarn: 900 (1000, 1100, 1200) yds or approx 7 (7, 8, 9) 1¾oz/50g balls taupe (for V-neck) or ivory (for round neck). 2 yd lengths of same yarn is used for cables.

Contrast colors (CC) Lengths in DK to Aran weight yarns in slightly lighter colors than MC such as lighter taupes to off-whites for V-neck version, creams to off-whites for round neck version; see table on next page for specific lengths.
A. Sizes 5 and 7 (3.75 and 4.5mm) needles, *or size to obtain gauge.*
B. Cable needle (cn).
C. Six ½" buttons in neutral color.

STITCH PATTERN

Tweed stitch (multiple of 2 sts)
Row 1 (RS) With CC, *sl 1 purlwise with yarn in front (wyif), k1; rep from*. **Row 2** With CC, purl. **Row 3** With MC, *k1, sl 1 purlwise wyif; rep from*. **Row 4** With MC, purl. Rep rows 1—4 for Tweed st pat, changing CCs every 28 rows.
Cable pat (over 4 sts inc d to 6 sts, then dec d to 4 sts)
Row 1 (RS) P1, k2, p1. **Row 2** K1, [p into front and back of next st] twice, k1 6 sts. **Rows 3** P1, sl 2 to cn and hold to back of work, k2; k2 from cn, p1. **Rows 4—8** K the knit sts and p the purl sts. **Rows 9—26** Rep rows 3—8 a total of 3 times. **Row 27** Rep row 3. **Row 28** K1, [p2tog] twice, k1 4 sts. Repeat rows 1—28 for Cable pat.

Note. Every 28 rows, Tweed st and Cable pats are offset; with a new cable positioned over center 4 sts of previous Tweed st section.

BACK

With smaller needles and MC, cast on 114 (118, 122, 126) sts. **Work edging** Work 4 rows rev St st [p on RS, k on WS], end with a WS row. Change to larger needles.
Establish pats as foll: Use first tier of drawing on next page as guide for pat and st placement. Beg with row 1 of Tweed st and Cable pats. **Beg pats: Row 1** (RS) K1 CC (selvage), work 18 (20, 22, 24) sts Tweed st in CC, *4 sts Cable in MC, 20 sts Tweed st in CC; rep from* to last 23 (25, 27, 29) sts, work 4 sts Cable in MC, 18 (20, 22, 24) sts Tweed st in CC, end k1 CC (selvage). **Row 2** (WS) P first and last st in CC and work rem sts in Tweed and Cable pats as established. Work 26 more pat rows, AT SAME TIME, dec 1 st each side every 12th row twice 110 (114, 118, 122) sts.
Alternate pats as foll: Change CCs. Foll 2nd tier of drawing, work 28 rows more in pat and dec 1 st each side every 12th row twice 106 (110, 114, 118) sts. Change CCs. Foll 3rd tier of drawing, work 28 rows more in pat and cont to dec 1 st each side every 12th row 3 times 100 (104, 108, 112) sts. Cont to alternate pats and change CCs every 28 rows while dec 1 st each side every 12th row 3 times more 94 (98, 102, 106) sts. Work even in pat as established until piece measures 17½ (18½, 19½, 19½)" from beg, end with a WS row.
Shape armhole
Cont pats, bind off 6 sts beg next 2 rows. Dec 1 st each

The Color Principles

- MC is darker than CCs. For the white garment, MC is cream. For the taupe garment, MC is a medium intensity taupe.
- For the taupe garment, CCs range from light taupes to off-whites. For the white garment, CCs are off-whites.

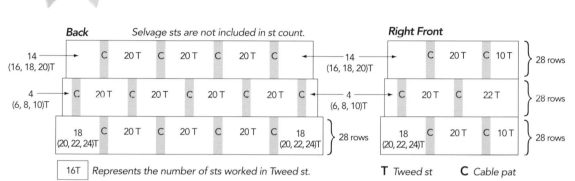

Back — Selvage sts are not included in st count. **Right Front**

| 16T | Represents the number of sts worked in Tweed st. |

T Tweed st **C** Cable pat

Length of CC required to work 28 rows	sts
1½ yds.	4 sts
2 yds.	6 sts
2½ yds.	8 sts
3 yds.	10 sts
3½ yds.	12 sts
4 yds.	14 sts
4½ yds.	16 sts
5 yds.	18 sts
5½ yds.	20 sts
6 yds.	22 sts
6½ yds.	24 sts

side every other row 8 (8, 8, 7) times—66 (70, 74, 80) sts. Work even until armhole measures 7½ (8, 8½, 9)" end with WS row. For round neck, mark center 28 sts. For V-neck, mark center 24 sts.

Round neck: Shape shoulder and neck
Bind off 4 (5, 5, 6) sts at beg of next 2 rows. **Next row** (RS) *Bind off 4 (5, 5, 6) sts, work to marked sts, turn. Bind off 1 st (neck edge), work to end.* Rep between *'s once. Bind off rem sts. Place center 28 sts on hold. With RS facing, join yarn to rem sts and work to end. Rep between *'s twice (binding off on WS rows for shoulder). Bind of rem sts.

V-neck: Shape shoulder and neck
Bind off 4 (5, 5, 6) sts at beg of next 2 rows. **Next row** (RS) *Bind off 5 (5, 6, 6) sts, work to marked sts, turn. Bind off 1 st (neck edge), work to end.* Rep between *'s once. Bind off rem sts. Place center 24 sts on hold. With RS facing, join yarn to rem sts and work to end. Rep between *'s twice (binding off on WS rows for shoulder). Bind off rem sts.

RIGHT FRONT
With smaller needles and MC, cast on 58 (60, 62, 64) sts. Work edging as for back. Change to larger needles. **Establish pats as foll** Use first tier of drawing as guide for pat and st placement. **Beg pats: Row 1** (RS) K1 CC (selvage), work 10 sts Tweed st in MC, 4 sts Cable in MC, 20 sts Tweed st in CC, 4 sts Cable in MC, 18 (20, 22, 24) Tweed st in CC, k1 CC (selvage). **Row 2** (WS) P first and last st in CC and work rem sts in Tweed and Cable pats as established. Work 26 more pat rows, AT SAME TIME, dec 1 st at side edge (end of RS row) every

12th row twice—56 (58, 60, 62) sts. **Alternate pats as foll** Change CCs. Foll 2nd tier of drawing, work 28 rows more in pats and dec 1 st at side edge every 12th row twice—54 (56, 58, 60) sts. Change CCs. Foll 3rd tier of drawing, work 28 more rows in pat and cont to dec 1 st at side edge every 12th row 3 times—51 (53, 55, 57) sts. Cont to alternate pats and change CCs every 28th row while dec 1 st at side edge every 12 rows 3 times more—48 (50, 52, 54) sts. **For round neck**, work even until piece measures same as back to armhole, end with a RS row. **For V-neck**, work even until piece measures 15½ (16½, 17½, 17½)" from beg, end with a WS row.

Round neck version
Shape armhole Shape armhole as for back—34 (36, 38, 41) sts. Work even until armhole measures 5½ (6, 6½, 7)", end with a WS row.

Shape neck: Next row (RS) Bind off 8 sts, work to end—26 (28, 30, 33) sts. At neck edge, bind off 3 sts once, 2 sts once, 1 st 4 times—17 (19, 21, 24) sts. Work even until armhole measures same as back to shoulder, end with a RS row.

Shape shoulder At shoulder edge, bind off 4 (5, 5, 6) sts 3 times. Bind off rem sts.

V-neck version
Shape neck: Next row (RS) Dec 1 st (neck edge), work to end—47 (49, 51, 53) sts.

Shape neck and armhole simultaneously as foll. Dec 1 st at neck every 4th row 14 times more, AT SAME TIME, when piece measures same as back to armhole, shape armhole as for back. After neck and armhole decs, work even on 19 (21, 23, 26) sts until armhole measures same as back to shoulder, end with a RS row.

TECHNIQUE NOTES
1. Twist yarns at CC changes to avoid holes.
2. Two of every four rows are worked in MC. Carry MC loosely up side of work.
3. Two of every four rows are worked in CC with MC cables. 2 yd lengths of MC are required to work cables on these CC rows.
4. Pattern contains options for V and round neck shaping.

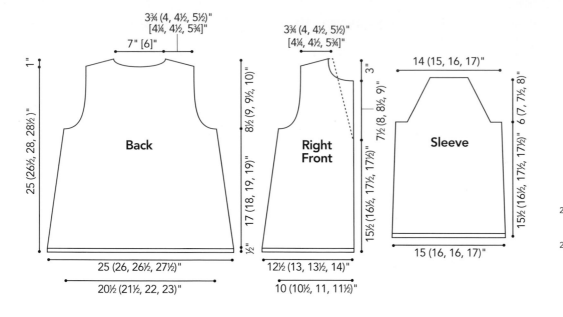

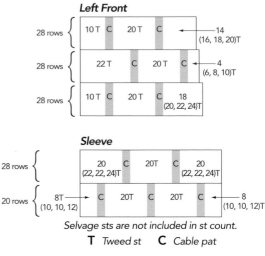

Selvage sts are not included in st count.

T Tweed st **C** Cable pat

Shape shoulder At shoulder edge, bind off 4 (5, 5, 6) sts once, 5 (5, 6, 6) sts twice. Bind off rem sts.

LEFT FRONT

With smaller needles and MC, cast on 58 (60, 62, 64) sts. Work edging as for back. Change to larger needles. **Establish pats as foll** Use first tier of drawing as guide for pat and st placement. **Beg pats: Row 1** (RS) K1 CC (selvage), work 18 (20, 22, 24) sts Tweed st in CC, 4 sts Cable in MC, 20 sts Tweed st in CC, 4 sts Cable in MC, 10 sts Tweed st in MC, k1 CC (selvage). Using left front drawing as guide, work to correspond to right front, dec at side edge and reversing armhole, neck and shoulder shaping.

SLEEVES

With smaller needles and MC, cast on 70 (74, 74, 78) sts. Work edging as for back. Change to larger needles. **Establish pats as foll** Use first tier of drawing as guide for pat and st placement. **Beg pats: Row 1** (RS) K1 CC (selvage), work 8 (10, 10, 12) sts Tweed st in MC, [4 sts Cable in MC, 20 sts Tweed st in CC] twice, 4 sts Cable in MC, 8 (10, 10, 12) sts Tweed st in CC, k1 CC (selvage). Work 19 more pat rows. Foll 2nd tier of drawing to off-set pats and **for sizes S, M only** dec 1 st each side every 40 rows twice—66 (70) sts rem. **For all sizes,** work even in pats as established, changing CCs after 28 rows and offsetting Tweed and Cable st pats until piece measures 15½ (16½, 17½, 17½)" from beg, end with a WS row.

Shape cap

Bind off 6 sts at beg of next 2 rows—54 (58, 62, 66) sts. *Dec 1 st each side of next 2 RS rows. Work 2 rows even. Rep from* until 22 sts rem. Bind off 2 sts at beg of next 2 rows. Bind off rem sts.

FINISHING

Block pieces. Sew shoulder seams. **For both versions,** work all bands as foll: With RS facing, smaller needles, and MC, pick up sts as instructed. Complete rev St st band by working [k 1 row, p 1 row] twice. Bind off all sts. After working bands, set in sleeves. Sew side and sleeve seams.

Round neck version

Neckband Beg at right front neck edge and pick up and k106 sts evenly around neck including sts on hold. Complete band.

Buttonband Beg at left front neck edge and pick up and k2 sts for every 3 rows to lower edge. Complete band. Sew 6 buttons between band and body, the first 1" from neck edge, the last 9" from lower edge, and 4 others spaced evenly between.

Buttonhole band Beg at lower right front edge and pick up and k2 sts for every 3 rows to neck edge, AT SAME TIME, work buttonholes by casting on 1 st (instead of picking up 1 st) opposite each button. Complete band.

V-neck version

Buttonband Beg at center back and k12 sts on hold, pick up and k5 sts along left back neck shaping, 3 sts for every 4 rows to point of V-neck, work k1, yo, k1 at point of V, 2 sts for every 3 rows to lower edge. Complete band. Sew 6 buttons between band and body, the first at point of V, the last 2" from lower edge, and 4 others spaced evenly between.

Buttonhole band Beg at lower right front edge and pick up and k2 sts for every 3 rows to point of V, AT SAME TIME, work buttonholes by casting on 1 st (instead of picking up 1 st) opposite each button; then cont to pick up and work k1, yo, k1 into st at point of V, 3 sts for every 4 rows from V to shoulder, 5 sts along back neck shaping, k12 sts on hold. Complete band. Sew bands tog at back neck.

Knitting as warp

I first saw and made a

garment from this technique

18 years ago. The original

was garter stitch except for

bands of woven stockinette

stitch across the chest.

After this first piece,

I made and sold similar

garments, often working on

my knitting machine and

from side to side so the

woven bands were vertical.

Three years ago, when I was

in early-book throes

a friend wore one of these

"blast-from-the-past"

sweaters. I looked at it and

wondered "What if I weave

the entire garment?"

The concept was so

exciting, I hardly slept.

It seemed that this technique—which I call Knitting as Warp—might be a good one for working through a yarn collection. My first attempt showed that it accommodated different yarn weights and integrated main and contrast colors beautifully.

I worked a more formal swatch and wrote the pattern for Tricia's Coat then took it to my trusted knitter, Stasia. A few days later I dropped by to see how it was going. What I saw astounded me! The fabric was stunning and was knitting up very quickly. Now I *really* couldn't sleep!

Over the next few months I continued to develop this technique—first another coat (The Shadow Box) then the simple Riley's "Jeans" Pullover, and then the more complex Kilim Coat Dress. Every piece was a delight, and this stitch pattern became the feature of the book that most excited me.

All I had to do was convince everyone else! It's an unfamiliar way of working, and it doesn't immediately inspire knitters to try it.

The base of these garments is worked in a main yarn and in *very loose* stockinette stitch, producing a piece of fabric that does not have enough body to be worn. This work is then used as warp, through which contrast yarns are woven, over and back on the same knitted row. All of the color work is done (woven) with contrasting yarns, following a chart, and after the garment is knit. (See p. 104 for weaving instructions)

So the first reaction is usually, "You mean you have to knit it *first* and *then* you weave it? Sounds like *way* too much work!"

Yes, it may sound like a great deal of work to first knit the fabric and then weave in the contrast colors, but consider how quickly the base fabric—or warp—is produced. There are simply not very many stitches! The back of Tricia's Coat is only 60 sts X 80 rows; if you average 40 sts per minute, this would take just two hours to knit!

Also, it's a way to produce very complex color work fairly simply because you only weave one contrast color at a time, rather than knitting them in and managing more than one color at a time (as you would with fairisle or intarsia).

This fabric also has an advantage that comes with any woven fabric—a firmness that wears well. Unless a coat or dress is knit very tightly, it may sag with wear or over time. This does not happen with the Knitting as Warp fabric: I have worn the Kilim Coat Dress through airplane flights and banquets without it "seating."

Besides all the advantages listed above, it is kind of fun to produce a fabric that confounds all your other fiber friends! ("It's not intarsia? It's slip stitch? No? Let me see the wrong side! What *is* this stuff?") The piece that puzzles them most is Shannon's Pullover because the latched verticals look exactly like knit stitches, which of course they are not.

Finally, Knitting as Warp might be a great beginner project for a young person learning to knit: the child works a piece on very large needles (for which perfect tension is not required) and then finishes the fabric by learning how to weave! Cool!

READING
CHARTS
A magnetic board is a
wonderful boon to
knitters. One student
said to me "Don't tell
my husband, but it
changed my life!"
The magnetized
board comes with
strips that stick to it.
When working from a
chart or from
complicated
knitting
instructions,
lay the board
behind the
page and the
strip on top of
the page, either
above or below
the row you are
working on.
You will no
longer be
searching for
your place
after you have
looked up
from the page
to knit.

How to weave using knitting as warp

Machine knitters might especially love the ability to produce this fabric in minutes. Try working on every second needle of your machine, and on a very loose tension. If you run out of needles, try *working 1, skipping 1, working 2, skipping 1; repeat from*.

DIRECTIONS

- Each row of weaving is accomplished by two passes with CC: the first is from right to left and the second is from left to right.
- Use a separate length of CC for each area.
- Work as directed whether right-handed or left-handed.
- Diagrams show a shaded selvage stitch. Only one-half of this stitch is shown; the other half rolls to the back.
- Thread a blunt tipped tapestry needle with CC.

1 Begin with needle coming from back of fabric through to front of fabric at right of first stitch you wish to weave.

a Working from right to left, pass needle under left half of this first stitch and out to front side of fabric between this stitch and the next

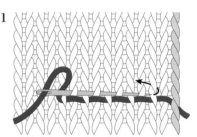

Continue passing needle over right half of each stitch and under left half of each stitch for all stitches to be woven with this CC on this row.

Turn by putting needle through to back at center of last stitch woven.

b Staying in same row of knit stitches and working from left to right, weave over other halves of stitches as follows: working above CC already woven, pass needle under right half of each stitch and over left half of each stitch for all stitches to be woven with this piece of CC.

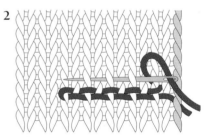

End with needle on front of fabric at right of first stitch woven.

2 To continue, take needle through to back of fabric, and bring through to front of fabric at right of next stitch to be woven. Repeat Steps 1a and 1b for each row of chart.

3 Diagram 3 shows our 3-row, 5-stitch triangle chart as it appears when woven.

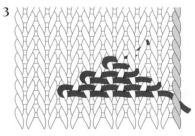

NOTES

- Each row of chart requires weaving over and back on the same row. Be careful to stay in the same knitted row. The second pass (from left to right) will be a little tighter than the first pass. If it is not, you may have moved up a row.
- Your color pattern is established with your weaving.
- Care must be taken to weave to a consistent tension. The CC should lie flat to the base fabric without pulling it out of shape.
- Once you have worked your first row (two passes, over and back) of weaving, you have established your gauge. Check to make sure it is correct.
- Once your gauge is established, it is not difficult to maintain especially since areas of weaving in these charts are over a short number of stitches.

You will be working from a chart. Each row of the chart is one knitted row and two passes of weaving. For example, here is the chart for our sample triangle.

Weaving chart

75

70

60

50

40

30

20

S ____
M ____
L ____

10

☐ LCC

▨ MCC

▩ DCC

1

14-sts

Ann's Purse

My editors suggested a small project to initiate knitters to the Knitting as Warp technique. The result is this purse, made from something not much larger than a tension swatch. I love the beaded purses, barely large enough to hold a quarter, a child's tooth, and a wedding ring. Ann Regis has said that a purse needs only be large enough to hold a credit card! The following is larger than both of these. It will hold what I see as essentials: a credit card, a phone card, a debit card, a couple of business cards, a key, paper and pen, and glasses. However, it can function more simply, without lining and/or strap.

DIFFICULTY	Beginner
SIZES	S (M, L) S is long enough for glasses pocket to hold a pair of clip-on shades, M is long enough for glasses pocket to hold a pair of small glasses, L is long enough for glasses pocket to hold a pair of large glasses. Model is shown in size S.
FINISHED MEASUREMENT	Width 4" Folded length 5½ (6⅜, 7¼)"
GAUGE	16 sts and 18 rows to 4"/10cm after weaving.

MATERIALS

Main color (MC) in DK weight yarn: approx 100 yds or 1 1¾oz/50g ball in dark green.

Contrast colors (CC) varying lengths in DK to Aran weight yarn: light intensity (LCC) yellow-oranges, medium intensity (MCC) yellow-greens, yellow-oranges, and browns, dark intensity (DCC) yellow-greens, greens, and browns.

B. Sizes 3 and 10 (3.25 and 6.5mm) needles, *or size to obtain gauge*

C. One pair size 3 (3.25mm) double-pointed needles (dpn).

D. One 1" button in CC.

E. Optional 5 (10, 10)" of 44" coordinating fabric for lining.

F. Optional 4" medium weight interfacing for lining.

PURSE

Upper edging With smaller needles and MC, cast on 21 sts. Work 3 rows in rev St st (p on RS, k on WS), end with WS row. **Base fabric** With larger needles and MC, work next row as follows: (RS) * k2, ssk, rep from* until 1 st rem, k1—16 sts. Beg with p row, work in St st to 59 (67, 75) rows (end with RS row). **Buttonhole flap edging** With smaller needles, bind off purlwise and as foll: p2, bind off 1 st, *p in front of next st on left hand needle and, without letting st on left hand needle drop, bind off 1 st, p in back of next st on left hand needle and, letting st on left hand needle drop, bind off 1 st, bind off 2 sts, rep from* until 1 st rem, p and bind off until 1 st rem on right hand needle. Draw ball of yarn through last st; do not break thread. Turn work. (RS facing): pick up and k 9 sts from back edge of bound-off row, turn, form buttonhole space by casting on 5 sts, turn, skip 3 bound-off sts, pick up and k 9 sts from back edge of bound-off row—23 sts. Work 3 rows in rev St st, ending with WS row. Bind off all sts purlwise; break thread.

Weave all sts except selvage sts according to chart and for size indicated.

FINISHING

Tack upper edging closed. Tack buttonhole flap edging closed, sewing bound-off edge to cast-on row for buttonhole space.

Side edgings Along both side edges, with smaller needles and MC, pick up and k2 sts along edge of upper and buttonhole flap edgings then 1 st for ea space (row) between selvage sts and woven fabric—63 (71, 79) sts. Work 4 rows in rev St st edging, ending with RS row. Bind off all sts. Tack side edgings closed.

Block piece to 4" X 12½ (14¼, 16)".

Strap With MC, make rev I-cord as follows. On dpn,

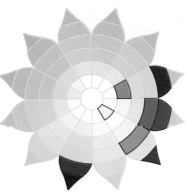

The Color Principles
- MC is darker than all CCs; for this piece, MC is dark yellow-green.
- All CCs are from warm side of the color wheel—from green to orange.
- CC1s are light intensity.
- CC2s are medium-light to medium-dark intensity.
- CC3s are dark intensity.

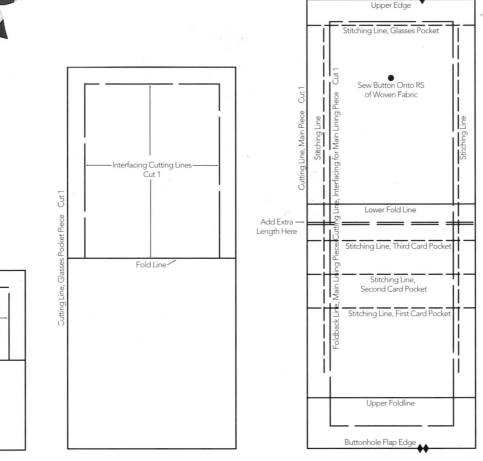

TECHNIQUE NOTES
1. The purse is worked in St st with MC, then woven with CCs following chart. You could use other charts in this section—Riley's Jeans Pullover or Tricia's Coat— if you prefer.
2. For weaving instructions, see discussion on p. 104.
3. Lining the purse is optional: sew sides together between fold lines for unlined purse. Do not work strap on unlined purse and it functions as a soft case for glasses.

cast on 5 sts. **Next row** k. **Next and all foll rows** wyif, sl all sts to other end of needle, pull working thread tight, k5; do not turn. (I-cord will now have rev St st side as RS.) Work to 33" or to desired length. Bind off all sts. Block and stretch to 39". (Cord will stretch approx one-fifth of its length.) Join cord ends tog. Attach to purse just under upper foldline.

LINING
Photostatically enlarge lining pattern pieces by 280% and onto 14" X 8½" paper—so length of main lining piece is 13¼". **M and L sizes only** Cut paper pattern along extra length line and add 1¾ (3½)" extra length.
Main piece Cut one piece from lining fabric along cutting lines. Cut one piece from interfacing along cutting lines.
Card pocket pieces Cut three pieces from lining fabric along cutting lines. Cut three pieces from interfacing fabric along cutting lines.
Glasses pocket lining piece Cut one piece from lining fabric along cutting lines. Cut one piece from interfacing fabric along cutting lines.

Attach interfacing For all pieces, attach interfacing to WS of lining as indicated in pattern pieces and according to manufacturer's directions.
Pockets Turn all pocket pieces right side out and press along foldlines.
Attach pockets to main piece With pockets against right side of main piece and rough edges towards buttonhole flap edge, sew along stitching lines. Fold all pockets up from stitching and towards buttonhole flap with third card pocket on top and first card pocket on bottom. Pin sides to main piece and sew along pocket side stitching lines, working from single notched edge towards double notched edge.
Attach lining to purse Turn all main lining piece edgings back along foldback line and press. Blind stitch lining to purse just inside of all rev st st edgings and with all pocket openings towards buttonhole flap.
Fold purse along upper and lower foldlines.
Sew button as indicated in paper pattern and to correspond to buttonhole space.

107

Shannon's Pullover

Shannon is my 14-year-old grandson. He has always been an artistic kid, so I made this "color exercise" garment for him. It required finding the full range of colors of the color wheel and moving around the wheel in regular steps. This is not as easy as it sounds, and that's why I call it an "exercise."

DIFFICULTY	Intermediate
SIZES	S (M, L, XL). Shown in size M.
FINISHED MEASUREMENTS	Chest 40½ (44, 48, 51½)" Length 24 (25½, 27, 28½)"
GAUGE	13 sts and 17 rows to 4"/10cm using larger needles and measured after weaving and latching.

MATERIALS

Main color (MC) in Aran weight yarn: 880 (1025, 1170, 1330) yds or approx 10 (12, 14, 16) 1¾oz/50g balls in black.

Contrast colors (CC) in DK, worsted, or Aran weight: approx 18 (18, 18, 20) 57" lengths each and 18 (18, 22, 22) 30" lengths each of 11 (12, 13, 14) colors covering the color wheel. Use tapestry yarns if you are missing a color or if you run out of a color.

A. Sizes 5 and 13 (3.75 and 7.5mm) needles, *or size to obtain gauge.*

B. Size G/6 (4.50mm) crochet hook.

BACK

With smaller needles and MC, cast on 85 (93, 101, 105) sts. Work 3" in k2, p2 rib (end k1 on RS row, beg p1 on WS row), end with a RS row. Change to larger needles.

Dec row (WS) P3 (1, 0, 5) *p2tog, p3; rep from* to last 2 (2, 6, 5) sts and **for sizes S, M only,** p2tog; **for size L,** p2tog, p2, p2tog; **for size XL,** p5—68 (74, 80, 86) sts. Work 86 (92, 98, 104) rows in St st. Mark center 22 sts.

Shape neck

Next row (RS) K23 (26, 29, 32), turn. Bind off 1 st

(neck edge), p to end—22 (25, 28, 31) sts. Turn and work 2 rows more on these sts only. Bind them off. Place center 22 sts on hold. With RS facing, join MC and k23 (26, 29, 32), turn. P 1 row, turn. Bind off 1 st, k to end. P 1 row more on rem 22 (25, 28, 31) sts, then bind off.

FRONT

Cast on and work rib as for back. Work dec row, then work 78 (84, 90, 96) rows in St st.

Shape neck

Next row (RS) K28 (31, 34, 37) sts, place center 12 sts on hold, join a 2nd ball of MC and k to end. Working both sides at same time, bind off from each neck edge 3 sts once, 1 st 3 times. Work 4 rows even—piece measures same as back to shoulder. Bind off all sts.

SLEEVES

With smaller needles and MC, cast on 37 (41, 45, 49) sts. Work 3" in k2, p2 rib (end k1 on RS row, beg p1 on WS row), end with a RS row. Change to larger needles. P 1 row and dec 5 (3, 7, 9) sts evenly across—32 (38, 38, 40) sts. Work 60 (66, 72, 78) rows in St st, AT SAME TIME, inc 1 st each side every 4th row 15 (14, 16, 18) times—62 (66, 70, 76) sts. Bind off all sts.

FINISHING

With 57" and 30" lengths of CCs, weave colors according to chart and notes in The Color Principles. With crochet hook at front of work and MC at back, beg at lower edge of weaving and fill holes produced in weaving by latching one chain stitch in each space up vertical line between colors (see Appendix, p. 138). Work for all ver-

The Color Principles

- MC is darker than CCs; for this garment, MC is black.
- CCs are in medium to medium-dark intensity and cover the wheel in regular, equal steps.
- Assign yellow to #8. This will insure this color, which attracts the eye most, remains at the center front of the body and does not appear on the sleeves.
- Any one of the 12 colors may be left out (because you don't like it or because you don't have any). To add colors (to get to the 13 or 14 required for the larger sizes or to fill in for a color that is missing) add a darker shade of any color used, and use it next to its lighter shade. For example, the model garment (which required 12 CCs), has a dark intensity blue (as #3) sitting next to a medium intensity blue (as #4).

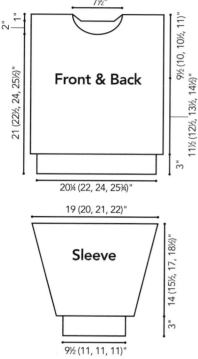

Front & Back

7½"

2"
1"

21 (22½, 24, 25¾)"

9½ (10, 10½, 11)"

11½ (12½, 13½, 14½)"

3"

20¼ (22, 24, 25¾)"

Sleeve

19 (20, 21, 22)"

14 (15½, 17, 18½)"

3"

9½ (11, 11, 11)"

ticals on front, back, and sleeves. Block pieces. Sew left shoulder seam.

Neckband

With RS facing, smaller needles, and MC, beg at back neck and pick up and k90 sts evenly around neck, including sts on hold. Work 7 rows in k2, p2 rib, end each RS row with k2 and beg each WS row with p2. Purl 1 row on RS for turning ridge. Work 6 rows more in k2, p2 rib as established. Bind off all sts. Fold neckband at turning ridge and tack to WS. **Optional:** With crochet hook at front of work and MC at back, fill holes around neck by latching one chain st in each space that appears around base of neck. Sew right shoulder seam, including neckband.

Place markers 9½ (10, 10½, 11)" down from shoulders on front and back. Sew top of sleeve between markers. Sew side and sleeve seams.

TECHNIQUE NOTES

1. Garment is worked in St st with MC, then woven with CCs following chart.
2. Schematic reflects measurements after weaving.
3. For weaving instructions, see discussion on p. 104.
4. First and last sts are selvage sts. Do not weave selvage sts; these sts are not included in the weaving chart.

Weaving chart, front and back

2	3	4	5	6	7	8	9	10	11	1 12	1 13	1 14	1
1	2	3	4	5	6	7	8	9	10	11	12	13	14
2	3	4	5	6	7	8	9	10	11	1 12	1 13	1 14	1
1	2	3	4	5	6	7	8	9	10	11	12	13	14
2	3	4	5	6	7	8	9	10	11	1 12	1 13	1 14	1
1	2	3	4	5	6	7	8	9	10	11	12	13	14
2	3	4	5	6	7	8	9	10	11	1 12	1 13	1 14	1
1	2	3	4	5	6	7	8	9	10	11	12	13	**14**
2	3	4	5	6	7	8	9	10	11	1 12	1 13	1 14	**1**
1	2	3	4	5	6	7	8	9	10	11	12	13	14
2	3	4	5	6	7	8	9	10	11	1 12	1 13	1 14	1
1	2	3	4	5	6	7	8	9	10	11	12	13	
1	2	3	4	5	6	7	8	9	10	11	12	13	

—— Small —— Medium —— Large —— X-large —— All sizes

Weaving chart, sleeve

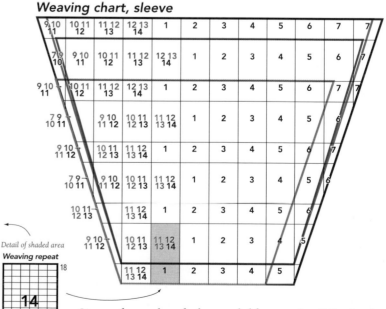

Detail of shaded area

Weaving repeat

18

14

10

1

6

14

1

6-sts

Line up the number of colors needed for your size. Following the color wheel, and giving yellow #8, assign each color of yarn a number from 1 to 11 (12, 13, 14). Then weave, following the chart.
Note *Where more than one number appears in a section, the color numbers are color-coded by size.*

Tricia's Coat

This coat was the first piece I designed in the Knitting as Warp technique. Soon after it was done I loaned it to my friend Tricia who was heading off to San Francisco for a week. It looked so good on her, we made a deal: I traded her the coat for a very large gift certificate at her wonderful bookstore, Words Worth Books, on King Street in Waterloo, Ontario, Canada. (A bookstore is the only commercial establishment besides a yarn shop out of which I cannot walk without a purchase!)

DIFFICULTY Intermediate

SIZES S (M, L, XL). Shown in size L.

FINISHED Bust 45 (48, 51, 54½)"
MEASUREMENTS Length 28½ (30, 31½, 33)"

GAUGE 10 sts and 11 rows to 4"/10cm using larger needles and measured after weaving.

MATERIALS

Main color (MC) in chunky weight yarn: 650 (760, 860, 990) yds or approx 6 (7, 8, 9) 3½oz/100g balls in dark blue.

Diagonal color (DC) in chunky weight or doubled DK/worsted weight yarn: 200 yds or two 3½oz/100g balls in darkest intensity blue.

Contrast colors (CC) in chunky weight yarn or doubled DK/worsted weight yarn: various lengths in medium to dark intensity red-purples, purples, blue-purples, blues, blue-greens, greens, and yellow-greens.

For pocket linings 30 yds MC or any CC in chunky weight yarn or 60 yds DK/worsted weight yarn, doubled.

A. Sizes 10 and 15 (6 and 10mm) needles, *or size to obtain gauge.*

B. Size 10 (6mm) circular needle, 29"/72cm (for front bands).

C. Five 1" buttons in CC.

BACK

With smaller needles and MC, cast on 54 (58, 62, 66) sts. K 6 rows. Change to larger needles. Work 72 (76, 80, 84) rows in St st, AT SAME TIME, inc 1 st each side every 12th row twice—58 (62, 66, 70) sts. Mark center 14 sts.

Shape shoulder and neck

Next row (RS) Bind off 7 (9, 9, 9) sts, k to marker, place 14 sts on hold, join a 2nd ball of MC and k to end. Working both sides at same time, shape shoulders by binding off 7 (9, 9, 9) sts at beg of next row, 7 (7, 8, 9) sts at beg of next 4 rows, AT SAME TIME, bind off 1 st from each neck edge once.

RIGHT FRONT

Pocket lining With yarn for lining and circular needle, cast on 21 sts. Working back and forth in rows, work 6" in St st, end with a WS row.

With smaller needles and MC, cast on 27 (29, 31, 33) sts. K 6 rows. Change to larger needles. Work a total of 58 (62, 66, 70) rows in St st, AT SAME TIME, inc 1 st at end of every 8th RS row twice—29 (31, 33, 35) sts.

Pocket placement After 30 (30, 36, 36) rows of St st, place pocket lining on RS row as foll: **Next row** (RS) K8 (10, 10, 12), place next 15 sts on hold, with RS facing, [k2tog, k2] 4 times across pocket lining, k2tog, k1, k2tog on rem pocket lining sts, then k to end. Cont in St st until required 58 (62, 66, 70) rows have been worked.

Shape neck and shoulder

Dec 1 st at beg of next (RS) row, then every other row 7 times more—21 (23, 25, 27) sts. Work even and when piece measures same as back to shoulder, shape shoulder as for back.

LEFT FRONT

Work as for Right front, including pocket lining, and reverse all shaping. **Reverse pocket placement: Next**

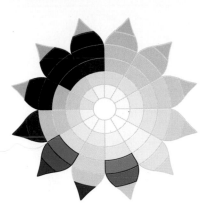

The Color Principles
- MC is medium-dark intensity; for this garment, MC is blue.
- DC is darkest intensity version of MC.
- CCs are medium to medium-dark intensity colors that cover one-half (in this case, the cool side) of the color wheel, with the inclusion of yellow-green.
- Variegated yarns, with greens, blues, purples, were used frequently.

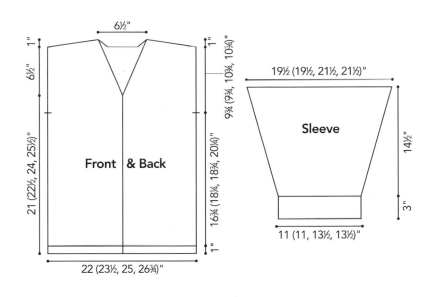

row (RS) K6 (6, 8, 8) sts, place next 15 sts on hold, with RS facing, [k2tog, k2] 4 times across lining, k2tog, k1, k2tog on rem pocket lining sts, then k to end.

SLEEVES
With smaller needles and MC, cast on 28 (28, 34, 34) sts. Work 3" in garter st. Change to larger needles. Work 42 rows in St st, AT SAME TIME, inc 1 st each side every 3rd row 11 times—50 (50, 56, 56) sts. Bind off all sts.

FINISHING
With DC, foll chart and weave diagonal lines. On sleeve weave above garter st cuff. With random lengths of CCs, weave spaces between diagonal lines.

Pocket edgings
With RS facing, smaller needles, and MC, pick up and k15 sts from holder and inc 6 sts evenly across—21 sts. K 6 rows. Bind off all sts.

Sew pocket linings to WS. Sew pocket edgings to RS. Block pieces. Sew shoulder seams.

TECHNIQUE NOTES
1. Garment is worked in St st with MC, then woven with DC and CC's following chart.
2. Schematic reflects measurements after weaving.
3. For weaving instructions, see discussion on p. 104
4. First and last sts are considered selvage sts. Do not weave selvage sts; these sts do not appear on charts.
5. Gaps may appear between woven fabric and edging; reinforce these by tacking together with MC on WS of work.

Left sleeve

Right sleeve

■ Diagonal color (DC)
□ Contrast color (CC)

▎Small, medium

▎Large, x-large

Weaving chart, left front, back, and right front

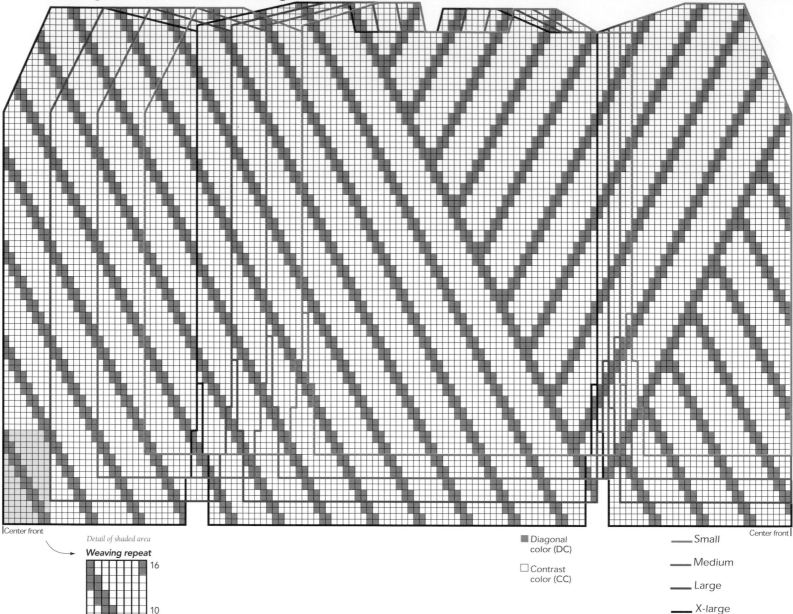

Center front

Detail of shaded area

Weaving repeat

16

10

1

8-sts

■ Diagonal color (DC)

□ Contrast color (CC)

—— Small

—— Medium

—— Large

—— X-large

Center front

Front bands and shawl collar

Row 1 With RS facing, circular needle, and MC, beg at lower right front edge and pick up and k1 st for every row to point of V-neck, work k1, yo, k1 into st at point of V, 3 sts for every 2 rows to shoulder, k24 sts from holder, 3 sts for every 2 rows along left front neck, work k1, yo, k1 into st at point of V, 1 st for every row to lower left front edge. **Row 2** Knit. **Row 3** K to 54 sts from point of V-neck, then work buttonholes as foll: *bind off 2 sts, k11; rep from* 4 times more, k to end. **Row 4** Knit and cast on 2 sts over each set of bound-off sts. **Rows 5–6** Knit.

Beg short rows for shawl collar: Row 1 Do not cut MC. Sl sts from left hand needle to right hand needle until 33 sts below right shoulder seam. Place marker,

join 2nd ball of MC and k33 sts from right front, 24 sts from back neck, then k33 sts from left front, place 2nd marker—90 sts just knit on right hand needle. Turn. **Row 2** Yo, sl first st, k to 3 sts from marker. Turn. **Row 3** Yo, sl first st, k to 3 sts from last yo. Turn. Rep row 3 until 27 sts rem (not including yo's) at each side and 24 rows have been worked at center back, end with a WS row. Cut yarn. With RS facing, sl sts so that they are all on LH needle and ready to beg work at lower right front edge. With MC, bind off all sts along right front to point of V, pick up and k all yo's along shawl collar and cont to bind off, then bind off all sts to end.

Sew buttons. Place markers 9¾ (9¾, 10¾, 10¾)" down from shoulders on front and back. Sew top of sleeves between markers. Sew side and sleeve seams.

Shadow Box Coat

To further explore the Knitting as Warp technique, I turned to quilting and a motif that produces an optical illusion from lights against darks. But this illusion does not show on the coat. I asked a quilting friend why, and she said that there was not enough contrast between the colors. The illusions seen in quilting depend upon contrast between lights and darks, and here the integration of the contrast colors with the main color had minimized this contrast. Oh well, maybe we don't want to walk around covered in optical illusions!

DIFFICULTY	Intermediate
SIZES	S (M, L, XL). Shown in size M.
FINISHED MEASUREMENTS	Bust 45 (48, 51, 54½)" Length 28½ (30, 31½, 33)"
GAUGE	10 sts and 11 rows to 4"/10cm using larger needles and measured after weaving.

Front & Back

6½"

1"

6½"

21 (22½, 24, 25½)"

9¾ (9¾, 10¾, 10¾)"

1"

16¾ (18¾, 18¾, 20¼)"

1"

22 (23½, 25, 26¾)"

Sleeve

19½ (19½, 21½, 21½)"

14½"

3"

11 (11, 13½, 13½)"

MATERIALS

Main colors (MC) In chunky weight yarn: 650 (760, 860, 990) yds or approx 6 (7, 8, 9) 3½oz/100g balls in dark brown.

Contrast colors (CC) In chunky weight yarn or doubled DK/worsted weight yarn: approx 65 lengths each as foll: 70" of charcoal grays or blacks (CC1), 50" of browns (CC2), 20" of dark red-purples (CC3), 90" of dark reds (CC4), 60" of medium intensity red-oranges (CC5), and 20" of medium intensity oranges and yellow-oranges (CC6).

Pocket linings In chunky weight yarn: 30 yds MC or any CC or 60 yds DK/worsted weight yarn, doubled

A. Sizes 10 and 15 (6 and 10mm) needles, *or size to obtain gauge.*

B. Size 10 (6mm) circular needle, 29"/72cm (for front bands).

C. Five 1" buttons in CC.

FOLL INSTRUCTIONS FOR TRICIA'S COAT, pp. 112-114.

The Color Principles
- MC is dark intensity; for this garment, MC is brown and darker than CC browns.
- CCs 3 through 6 are medium to dark intensity colors that cover nearly one-half of the color wheel; for this garment, these are red-purple to yellow-orange.
- CCs 1 and 2 are dark neutrals; for this garment, these are charcoal gray and brown.

Weaving repeat

15-sts

Weaving chart, right front

Left front

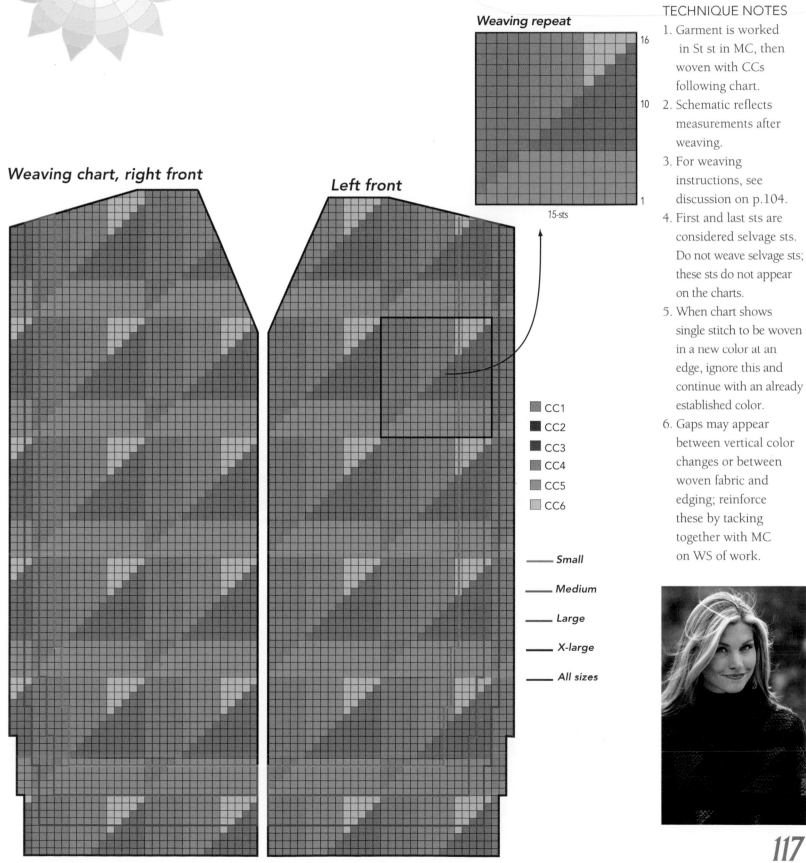

■ CC1
■ CC2
■ CC3
■ CC4
■ CC5
■ CC6

——— *Small*

——— *Medium*

——— *Large*

——— *X-large*

——— *All sizes*

TECHNIQUE NOTES
1. Garment is worked in St st in MC, then woven with CCs following chart.
2. Schematic reflects measurements after weaving.
3. For weaving instructions, see discussion on p.104.
4. First and last sts are considered selvage sts. Do not weave selvage sts; these sts do not appear on the charts.
5. When chart shows single stitch to be woven in a new color at an edge, ignore this and continue with an already established color.
6. Gaps may appear between vertical color changes or between woven fabric and edging; reinforce these by tacking together with MC on WS of work.

Weaving chart, back

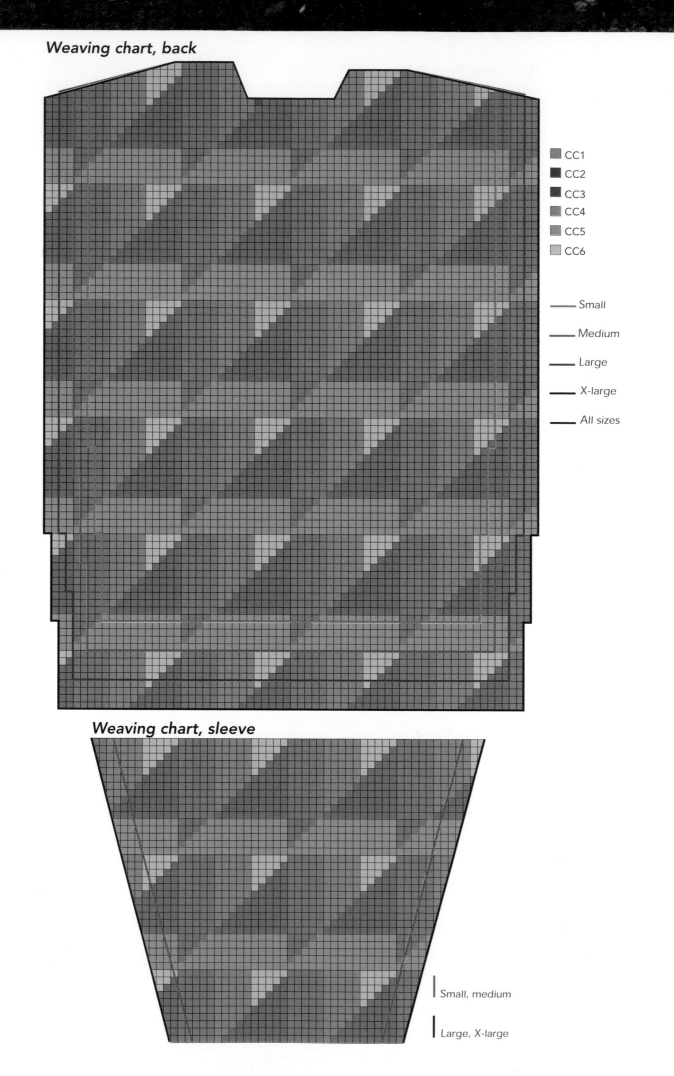

CC1
CC2
CC3
CC4
CC5
CC6

—— Small
—— Medium
—— Large
—— X-large
—— All sizes

Weaving chart, sleeve

| Small, medium

| Large, X-large

118

Riley's "Jeans" Pullover

Riley is my youngest grandson who was much smaller when I made this garment for him. Unfortunately, the garment's been travelling a bit with me and for my classes, so he hasn't had a chance to wear it, and it won't come close to fitting him now. (Haven't I said this somewhere before?!) It's a good thing these pieces work up quickly so I can make him a larger one!

DIFFICULTY	Beginner
SIZES	XS (S, M, L, XL) to fit child's sizes 2-4 (6, 8-10, 12, 14-16). Shown in size S.
FINISHED MEASUREMENTS	Chest 26 (30, 34, 38, 42)" Length 14 (16, 19, 22, 24)"
GAUGE	16 sts and 18 rows to 4"/10cm, using larger needles and measured after weaving.

MATERIALS

Main colors (MC) in DK weight yarn: 400 (500, 680, 880, 1050) yds or approx 3 (4, 5, 7, 8) 1¾oz/50g balls in medium-dark blue-green.

Contrast colors (CC) various lengths of sport, DK, and worsted weight yarns in light to medium-light intensity blues, blue-greens, greens, yellow-greens, yellows, yellow-oranges, oranges, and beiges.

A. Sizes 3 and 10½ (3.25 and 6.5mm) needles, *or size to obtain gauge.*

BACK

With smaller needles and MC, cast on 70 (82, 90, 102, 114) sts. Work 2 (2, 2, 3, 3)" in k2, p2 rib, end each RS row with k2 and beg each WS row with p2. Change to larger needles. **Next (dec) row** (RS) K3 (1, 5, 3, 1), *k2tog, k2; rep from* to last 3 (1, 5, 3, 1) sts, k3 (1, 5, 3, 1)—54 (62, 70, 78, 86) sts. Work 53 (63, 75, 85, 93) rows more in St st. Bind off 15 (19, 22, 25, 28) sts at beg of next 2 rows. Place rem 24 (24, 26, 28, 30) sts on hold.

FRONT

Cast on and work rib and dec row as for back. Work 41 (51, 63, 71, 79) rows more in St st.

Shape neck

Shaping takes place over 8 (8, 8, 10, 10) rows as foll: **Next row** (RS) K21 (25, 28, 32, 35), place next 12 (12, 14, 14, 16) sts on hold, join a 2nd ball of MC, k to end. Working both sides at same time, bind off from each neck edge 2 sts twice, 1 st 2 (2, 2, 3, 3) times—15 (19, 22, 25, 28) sts rem each side. Work 4 rows even. Bind off all sts.

SLEEVES

With smaller needles and MC, cast on 34 (34, 38, 42, 46) sts. Work 2 (2½, 3, 3, 3)" in k2, p2 rib as for back. Change to larger needles. **Next row** (RS) Knit and dec 2 (2, 2, 2, 6) sts evenly across—32 (32, 36, 40, 40) sts. Work 51 (55, 59, 63, 71) rows more in St st, AT SAME TIME, inc 1 st each side every 4th row 10 (12, 12, 12, 16) times—52 (56, 60, 64, 72) sts. Work even until piece measures 12 (14, 16, 17½, 20)" from beg. Bind off all sts.

FINISHING

Weave with lengths of CCs following chart and changing colors randomly. Block pieces. Sew left shoulder.

Neckband

With RS facing, smaller needles, and MC, pick up and k86 (90, 94, 98, 102) sts evenly around neck edge, including sts on hold. Work 7 rows in k2, p2 rib. Purl 1 row on RS for turning ridge. Work 5 rows more in rib. Bind off all sts.

Sew right shoulder, including neckband. Fold neckband at turning ridge and tack to WS. Place markers 6½ (7, 7½, 8, 9)" down from shoulders on front and back. Sew top of sleeves between markers. Sew side and sleeve seams.

The Color Principles
- MC is medium-dark intensity and darker than CCs; for this garment, MC is blue-green.
- CCs are medium-light and light intensity colors from one half the color wheel—for this garment, the bottom half, orange to blue.

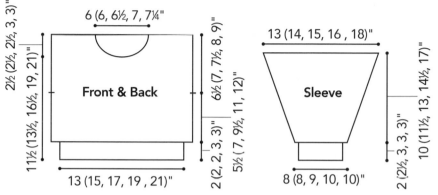

Front & Back

6 (6, 6½, 7, 7¼)"

2½ (2½, 2½, 3, 3)"

11½ (13½, 16½, 19, 21)"

6½ (7, 7½, 8, 9)"

2 (2, 2, 3, 3)"

5½ (7, 9½, 11, 12)"

13 (15, 17, 19, 21)"

Sleeve

13 (14, 15, 16, 18)"

10 (11½, 13, 14½, 17)"

2 (2½, 3, 3, 3)"

8 (8, 9, 10, 10)"

Weaving chart

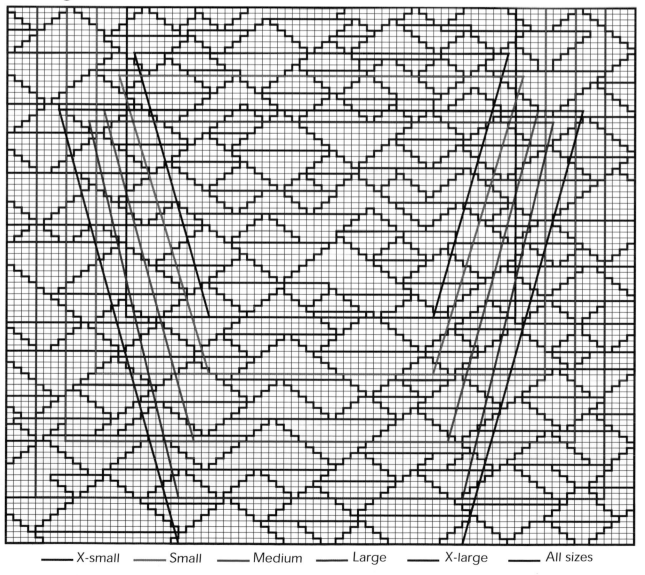

—— X-small —— Small —— Medium —— Large —— X-large —— All sizes

TECHNIQUE NOTES
1. Garment is worked in St st with MC, then woven with CCs following chart.
2. Schematic reflects measurements after weaving.
3. For weaving instructions, see discussion on p. 104.
4. First and last sts are selvage sts. Do not weave selvage stitches; these sts do not appear on the chart.
5. Gaps may appear between woven fabric and edging. Reinforce these by tacking together with MC.

Kilim Coat Dress

Years ago, while at the dentist, I saw a wonderful Kilim couch fabric in a decorating magazine. The dentist's wife was a knitter, so she allowed me to remove the page. I carried it around for years but never knit it up. Too complex! But then Knitting as Warp developed and seemed the perfect vehicle to simplify the work of reproducing this complicated pattern.

To choose a color combination, I went to a photo of a favorite painting, Paul Klee's "Ancient Sound, Abstract on Black" (1925), and found yarns in my collection that copied his colors then I divided them between lights, mediums, and darks to make the tapestry pattern work.

DIFFICULTY Intermediate

SIZES S (M, L, XL). Shown in size M.

FINISHED MEASUREMENTS Bust 40 (42, 45, 48)"
Length 31 (33, 34½, 36)"

GAUGE 16 sts and 18 rows to 4"/10cm in St st with largest needles, measured after weaving.
28 sts and 28 rows to 4"/10cm in k2, p2 rib with middle size needle, measured after lightly stretching and blocking.

MATERIALS

Main color (MC) in DK weight yarn: 1400 (1600, 1760, 2060) yds or approx 10 (12, 13, 15) 1¾oz/50g balls in black.

Contrast colors (CC) DK or worsted weight yarns in the foll: 1 yd lengths of light to light-medium intensity (LCC) yellow-greens, yellows, and yellow-oranges; 2½ yd lengths of medium to dark intensity (MCC) yellows, yellow-oranges, oranges, and red-oranges; 6½ yd lengths of dark intensity (DCC) blue-greens, greens, yellow-greens, yellows, yellow-oranges, oranges, red-oranges, reds, and red-purples.

A. Sizes 3, 5 and 10½ (3.25, 3.75 and 6.5mm) needles, *or size to obtain gauge.*

B. Six ⅝" buttons in MC.

BACK

With smallest needles and MC, cast on 104 (108, 118, 128) sts. Work 4 rows in rev St st [p on RS, k on WS], end with WS row. Change to largest needles. **Next row** (RS) K0 (2, 2tog, 2tog), *k2tog, k2; rep from* to last 0 (2, 0, 6) sts and **for sizes M, L only** k rem sts; **for size XL only** k2tog 3 times—78 (82, 88, 94) sts. Work 29 (31, 33, 35) rows more in St st. Cast on 2 sts at beg of next two rows—82 (86, 92, 98) sts. Work even until a total of 88 (92, 98, 102) rows in St st have been completed.

Shape armhole

Work a total of 36 (40, 42, 44) rows more as foll: Bind off 4 sts at beg of next 2 rows—74 (78, 84, 90) sts. Dec 1 st each side every other row 10 (10, 11, 12) times—54 (58, 62, 66) sts. Work even until required rows have been worked—124 (132, 140, 146) rows from beg. Bind off all sts.

RIGHT FRONT

With smallest needles and MC, cast on 53 (56, 60, 64) sts. Work rev St st edging as for back. Change to largest needles. **Next row** (RS) Work k2, k2tog across and dec to 40 (42, 45, 48) sts. Work 29 (31, 33, 35) rows more. Cast on 2 sts at beg of next row (side edge)—42 (44, 47, 50) sts. Work even until 89 (93, 99, 103) rows have been completed in St st, end with a RS row.

Shape armhole

Work a total of 35 (39, 41, 43) rows more as foll: **Next row** (WS) Bind off 4 sts, p across—38 (40, 43, 46) sts. Dec 1 st at armhole every other row 10 (10, 11, 12) times—28 (30, 32, 34) sts. Work even until required rows have been worked—124 (132, 140, 146) rows from beg. Bind off all sts.

LEFT FRONT

Work as for right front, reversing all shaping.

The Color Principles
- MC is darker than CCs; for this garment, MC is black.
- CCs are in 3 groups: light (LCC), medium (MCC), and dark (DCC).
- CCs cover just over one-half the color wheel (in this case, the warm side, from green to red with the addition of blue-green and red-purple).
- While the weaving pattern generally has the lightest colors in the center (over the smallest area), with the medium colors next and with the darkest colors to the outside (over the largest area), every once in a while it is a good idea to alternate the light with the medium, perhaps two or three times on each garment piece. This saves the piece from looking "spotty."

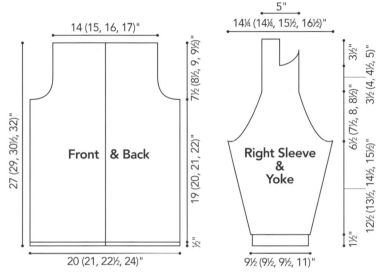

Front & Back
14 (15, 16, 17)"
7½ (8½, 9, 9½)"
19 (20, 21, 22)"
27 (29, 30½, 32)"
20 (21, 22½, 24)"
½"

Right Sleeve & Yoke
5"
14¼ (14¼, 15½, 16½)"
3½"
3½ (4, 4½, 5)"
6½ (7½, 8, 8½)"
12½ (13½, 14½, 15½)"
1½"
9½ (9½, 9½, 11)"

TECHNIQUE NOTES
1. Garment is worked in St st with MC, then woven with LCCs. MCCs, and DCCs following chart.
2. Schematic reflects measurements after weaving.
3. For weaving instructions, see discussion on p. 104.
4. First and last sts are selvage sts. Do not weave selvage st; these sts do not appear on the chart.
5. Gaps may appear between woven fabric and edging; reinforce these by tacking together with MC on WS of work.

RIGHT SLEEVE & YOKE
With smallest needles and MC, cast on 46 (46, 46, 54) sts. **Rows 1, 3** (WS) Knit. **Rows 2, 4** Purl. **Row 5** (WS) Purl and inc 7 sts evenly across—53 (53, 53, 61) sts. **Rows 6–11** Work in k2, p2 rib (end RS row with k1, beg WS row with p1). **Rows 12, 13, 15** Knit. **Rows 14, 16** Purl. Change to middle size needles. **Next row** (WS) Purl and inc 15 sts evenly across—68 (68, 68, 76) sts. **Next row** (RS) K5, *p2, k2, rep from* to last 7 sts, end p2, k5. Work 3 rows more in rib as established. **Next (inc) row** (RS) K3, inc 1 st purlwise, k2, work in rib across to last 5 sts, k2, inc 1 st purlwise, k3. Cont rib, AT SAME TIME, inc 1 st each side (working incs after first and before last k3 and working incs into rib pat) 16 (16, 20, 20) times—100 (100, 108, 116) sts. Rib pat at completion of incs should be k5, (p2, k2) across, end k3. Work even until piece measures 14 (15, 16, 17)" from beg, end with a WS row.

Shape cap
Bind off 8 sts at beg of next 2 rows—84 (84, 92, 100) sts. Cont in rib as established, AT SAME TIME, cont to dec 1 st at beg and end of every RS row as foll: K3, ssk, rib to last 5 sts, end k2tog, k3. Rep dec row until 36 sts rem.

Shape yoke
Work 3½ (4, 4½, 5)" even in rib across 36 sts, end with a WS row. **Shape front neck: Next row** (RS) Cont rib,

work 18 sts, place rem 18 sts on hold for back neck; turn and bind off next 5 sts (front neck edge), work to end. Cont rib and bind off from front neck edge 3 sts once, 2 sts twice, 1 st 5 times. Fasten off last st. **Shape back neck** Sl 18 sts on hold to needle. With RS facing, join yarn, bind off 1 st (neck edge) and rib to end. Bind off 1 st at neck edge once more, then work 3½" even on rem 16 sts. Place sts on hold.

LEFT SLEEVE & YOKE
Work as for right sleeve and yoke, reversing neck shaping.

FINISHING
Foll chart and notes in The Color Principles, weave fronts and back. Block pieces. Graft 16 sts of each back yoke tog. Matching center of yoke to center of back, sew yoke to back. Ending front yokes 1¼" from front edges, sew yoke to fronts. Sew sleeve seams. Sew side seams to top of vent openings.

Trim
At side vents With RS facing, smallest needles, and MC, pick up and k5 sts for every 4 rows along vent openings. K 1 row, p 1 row, then k 1 row. Bind off all sts purlwise. Sew trim closed at upper and lower edges.
At neck Beg at right front neck and pick up and k98 sts evenly around neck. Work trim as for vents.

123

Buttonband

With RS facing, smallest needles, and MC, beg at left front neck edge and pick up and k6 sts for every 5 rows to lower edge. **Rows 1, 3** (WS) Knit. **Row 2** Purl. **Row 4** (RS) Knit. **Row 5** Purl and inc in every 4th st across. **Rows 6–8** Work in k2, p2 rib. **Row 9** Purl, working every 4th and 5th st tog. **Row 10** Purl. **Rows 11–12** Rep rows 1–2. Bind off all sts knitwise.

Sew 5 buttons to center of rib, the first 1" from upper edge, the last 8 (9, 10, 11)" from lower edge, and 3 others spaced evenly between.

Buttonhole band

Beg at lower edge of right front and work as for buttonband, working 3-row buttonholes in rows 6–8 opposite buttons.

Weaving chart, back & front

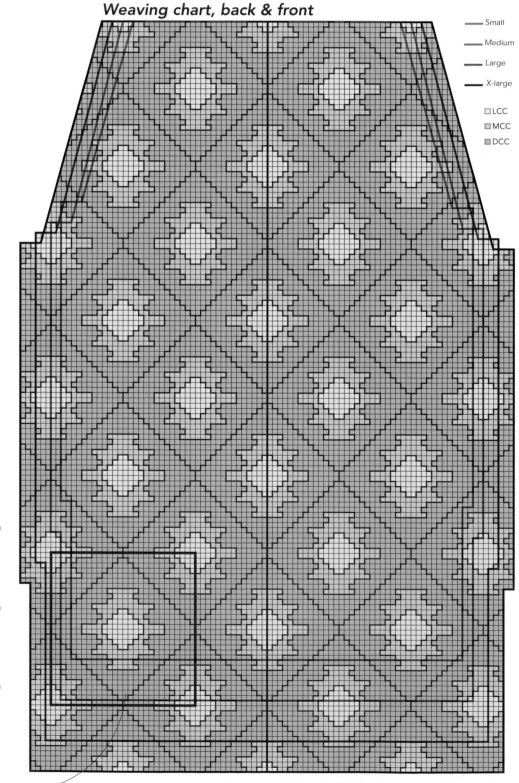

— Small
— Medium
— Large
— X-large

☐ LCC
☐ MCC
☐ DCC

Weaving detail

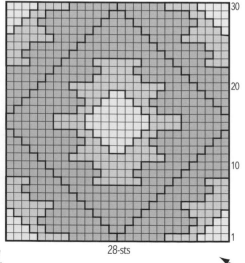

30
20
10
1

28-sts

Kilim Vest

After finishing the Kilim Coat Dress, I showed it to my hairdresser, Gudrun. She thought it very beautiful and asked if it would make up into a vest that could be worn instead of a coat during a Canadian spring and fall. I thought it would and then knit one. It seemed a lovely and practical garment, so I repeated it here for the book, using the same kilim chart as the coat dress but in another shape, yarn weight, color-way.

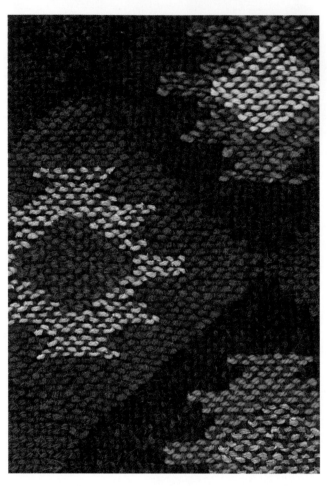

DIFFICULTY Intermediate

SIZES XS (S, M, L, XL). Shown in size M.

FINISHED Bust 39 (42½, 46, 49½, 53)"
MEASUREMENTS Length 30 (31, 32, 33, 34)"

GAUGE 13½ sts and 15½ rows to 4"/10cm using larger needles and measured after weaving.

MATERIALS

Main colors (MC) in Aran weight yarn: 570 (640, 700, 780, 860) yds or approx 7 (8, 8, 9, 10) 1¾oz/50g balls in medium to dark intensity brown.
Contrast colors (CC) DK to Aran weight yarns in the foll: 1 yd lengths of light intensity (LCC) red-oranges, oranges, yellow-oranges, yellows, yellow-greens, beiges, and off-whites; 2½ yd lengths of light-medium intensity (MCC) oranges, yellow-oranges, yellow-greens, greens, and blue-greens; 6¼ yd lengths of dark intensity (DCC) oranges, yellow-oranges, yellows, and yellow-greens.

For pocket linings 30 yds MC or any CC in Aran weight yarn.
A. Sizes 6 and 10½ (4 and 6.5mm) needles, *or size to obtain gauge.*
B. Size 6 (4mm) circular needle, 29"/72cm.
C. Five 1" buttons in MC.

BACK

With smaller needles and MC, cast on 64 (70, 76, 82, 88) sts. K 6 rows. Change to larger needles. Work 68 (72, 76, 80, 84) rows in St st and inc 1 st each side every 18th row twice—68 (74, 80, 86, 92) sts.

Shape armhole

Work 40 rows more as foll: Bind off 6 sts at beg of next 2 rows—56 (62, 68, 74, 80) sts. Dec 1 st each side every other row 5 times—46 (52, 58, 64, 70) sts. Work even until required rows have been worked—108 (112, 116, 120, 124) rows from beg. Mark center 18 sts.

Shape neck

Next row (RS) K14 (17, 20, 23, 26) sts, place center 18 sts on hold, join a 2nd ball of MC and k to end. Working both sides at same time, work 3 rows more, dec 1 st at each neck edge once. Bind off rem sts.

RIGHT FRONT

Pocket lining With yarn for lining and circular needle, cast on 24 sts. Working back and forth in rows, work 6" in St st, end with a WS row.
With smaller needles and MC, cast on 33 (36, 39, 42, 45) sts. K 6 rows. Change to larger needles. Work 69 (73, 77, 81, 85) rows in St st and inc 1 st at end of every 18th row twice—35 (38, 41, 44, 47) sts.
Pocket placement After 36 (40, 40, 44, 44) rows St st, place pocket lining on RS row as foll: **Next row** (RS) K9 (10, 12, 13, 15), place next 18 sts on hold, with RS facing, k 24 sts of pocket lining and dec 6 sts evenly across to 18 sts, k to end. Cont in St st until required 69 (73, 77, 81, 85) rows have been worked.

Shape armhole and neck

Work 39 rows more as foll: **Next row** (WS) Bind off 6 sts, p to end—29 (32, 35, 38, 41) sts. Dec 1 st at armhole every other row 5 times, AT SAME TIME, after working 3 rows, beg neck shaping by dec 1 st at neck edge every 3rd row 11 times—13 (16, 19, 22, 25) sts rem. Work even until piece measures same as back to shoulder—112 (116, 120, 124, 128) rows from beg. Bind off all sts.

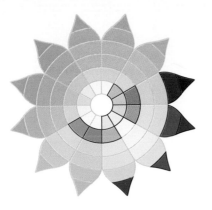

The Color Principles

- MC is a medium to dark intensity neutral; for this garment, MC is brown.
- CCs are in 3 groups: light (LCC), medium (MCC), and dark (DCC).
- CCs cover just over one-half the color wheel (in this case, the warm side, from blue-green to red-orange).
- While the weaving pattern generally has the lightest colors in the center (over the smallest area), with the medium colors next and the darkest colors to the outside (over the largest area), every once in a while it is a good idea to alternate the light with the medium, perhaps two or three times on each garment piece. This saves the piece from looking "spotty."

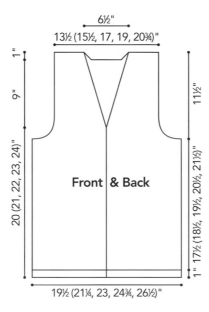

6½"
13½ (15½, 17, 19, 20¾)"
1"
9"
20 (21, 22, 23, 24)"
11½"
1" 17½ (18½, 19½, 20½, 21½)"

Front | & Back

19½ (21¼, 23, 24¾, 26½)"

TECHNIQUE NOTES

1. Garment is worked in St st with MC, then woven with LCCs, MCCs, and DCCs following chart.
2. Schematic reflects measurements after weaving.
3. For weaving instructions, see discussion on p. 104.
4. First and last sts are selvage sts. Do not weave selvage stitches; these sts do not appear on the chart.
5. Gaps may appear between woven fabric and edging; reinforce these by tacking together with MC on WS of work.

LEFT FRONT

Work as for right front, reversing all shaping. Work 68 (72, 78, 80, 84) rows in St st to armhole and 40 rows to shoulder.

FINISHING

Weave with CCs foll chart and notes in The Color Principles.

Pocket edging

With RS facing, smaller needles, and MC, pick up and k18 sts from holder and inc 6 sts evenly across—24 sts. K 6 rows. Bind off all sts. Sew pocket linings to WS. Sew pocket edgings to RS. Sew shoulder seams.

Front bands

With RS facing, circular needle, and MC, beg at lower right front edge and pick up and k as foll: 1 st per row to point of V-neck, work k1, yo, k1 into st at point of V, 7 sts per 6 rows to shoulder, 40 sts along back neck (including sts on hold), 7 sts per 6 rows to point of V-neck, work k1, yo, k1 into st at point of V, 1 st per row to lower edge of left front. **Rows 1–9** Knit and work buttonholes on row 5 as foll: k to 54 sts from point of V, then *bind off 2 sts, k 11 sts; rep from* 4 times more, k

to end. On row 6, cast on 2 sts over each set of bound-off sts. **Beg shawl collar: Row 1** (RS) Leave MC attached and sl sts to right hand needle until 56 sts from right shoulder seam. Place marker, join 2nd ball of MC and k56 sts to shoulder, k40 sts from back neck, k56 sts along left front—152 sts knit on right hand needle. Place marker and turn. **Row 2** Yo, sl first st, k until 5 sts from marker, turn. **Row 3** Yo, sl first st, k to 5 sts from last yo, turn. Rep row 3 until 45 sts are left (not including yo's) on each side and 32 rows have been worked at center back, end with a WS row. Cut yarn. With RS facing, sl sts, so that they are all on left hand needle and ready to beg work at lower right front edge. With MC, bind off all sts along right front to point of V, pick up and k all yo's along shawl collar and cont to bind off, then bind off all sts to end. Sew buttons opposite buttonholes.

Armbands

With RS facing, smaller needles, and MC, beg at underarm and pick up and k1 st for every bound-off st and 1st per row around armhole. K 5 rows. Bind off all sts. Sew side seams, including armbands.

Weaving chart, back & front

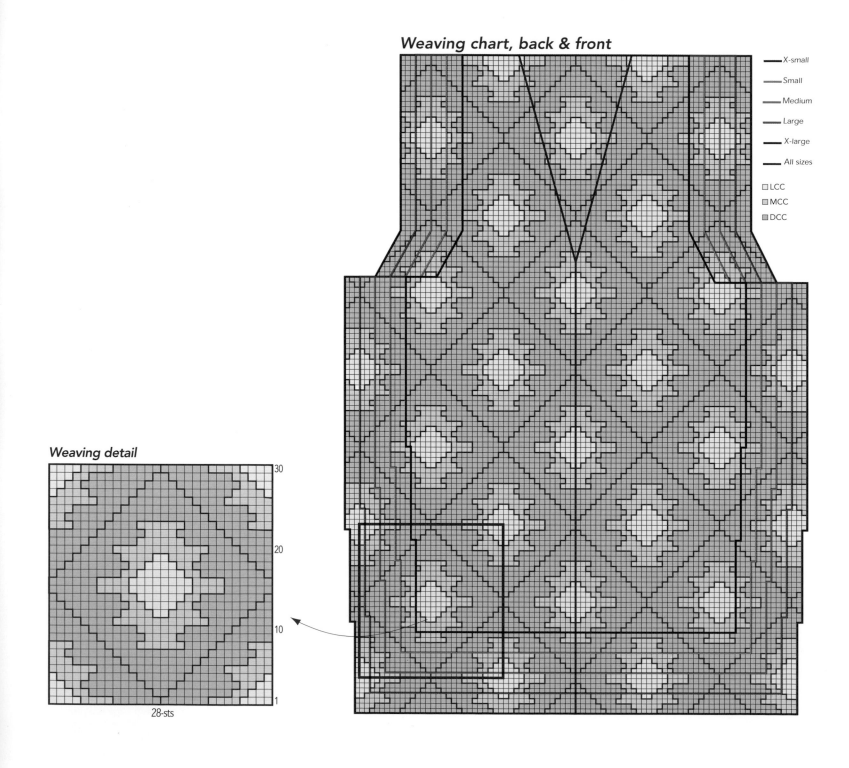

X-small
Small
Medium
Large
X-large
All sizes

☐ LCC
◪ MCC
◪ DCC

Weaving detail

30

20

10

1

28-sts

Basic Pattern Drafting

Horizontal

Number of stitches

Vertical

Number of rows

Diagonal

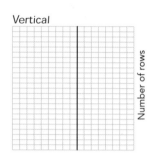

Number of stitches

Number of rows

Curve

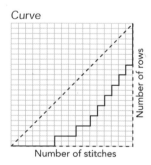

Number of stitches

Number of rows

Before you begin to work with the following material, let's start with an understanding of pattern drafting's basic principles.

- **A horizontal line is a number of stitches:** number of stitches in one inch times (X) desired number of inches equals (=) required number of stitches.

- **A vertical line is a number of rows:** number of rows in one inch X desired number of inches = required number of rows.

- **A diagonal line is a number of stitches, increased or decreased evenly over a number of rows.** Draw lines to get horizontal and vertical measurements, translate these to # of sts and rows, then divide larger number by smaller to get rate of increase or decrease, adjusting if you need to get a rate that is easy to work with—for example 3.2 can become 3 (dec 1 st every 3 rows).

- **A curve is a diagonal line (a number of stitches either increased or decreased over a number of rows) that is worked unevenly**—by increasing or decreasing more stitches at once at the beginning, then fewer stitches at a time in the middle, then none at all in the end (just a straight line).

Note. All that follows is geared toward pieces for garments worked flat, rather than in the round. What would you do differently if you were figuring for garments worked in the round? After determining desired bust measurement, you wouldn't divide by two (for front and back garment piece widths) nor allow for selvages on body or sleeves.

THE DROP SHOULDER PULLOVER

This style has a front, a back, and two sleeves. Although it is possible to work the front and back all in one piece—up the front and over the back, without shoulder seams—most stitch patterns don't look the same worked right-side-up as right-side-down. I also like the stability that seams give at the shoulders.

Front and back pieces to neck shaping

Until neck shaping, both front and back pieces are the same.

1. The Measurements

Because this style is not fitted, it is usually worked generously large. This comes as a shock to some knitters, but the finished bust measurement should be at least 6" larger than the actual bust measurement. I generally make mine 8" larger for a drop shoulder pullover. If you feel unsure, check the measurement of a drop shoulder garment you like the fit of. The bust measurement is then divided by two for the front and back width. This measurement is the body width

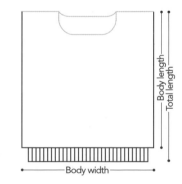

Body length
Total length

Body width

The only other measurement you need is your total length (body length plus length of edging). Although this can vary greatly, a standard body length is a bit longer (1 to 2") than the front or back width with an edging length of 3–4". There are many exceptions to this guideline for length so, again, check against an existing garment of approximately the same size. (If you think you might want something considerably shorter, fold up the existing garment and try it on, making sure to take a look at yourself from the back!)

2. The Calculations

- Measure across your swatch for the number (#) of stitches in 4"; do not round up or down.

- Divide this # by 4 = # of stitches in 1"; do not round up or down. This is your **stitch gauge**, or **gauge**.

- Measure your swatch for # of rows in 4"; do not round up or down.

- Divide this # by 4 = # of rows in 1"; do not round up or down. This is your **row gauge**.

- Determine the body width you want: (bust measurement + at least 6") divided by 2 = body width.

- Multiply this # of inches by the gauge = # of stitches in body width; round up or down to a whole number.

- Do you need to adjust this # of stitches to accommodate stitch or color pattern repeats?

- Add 2 selvage stitches.

- Determine # of stitches for bottom band (ribbing is often worked over 10–15% fewer stitches).

- Determine total length of garment: body length + length of edging = total length of garment.

3. The Pattern

With smaller needles, cast on # of stitches for bottom band; work to desired length, ending with RS row. **Next row** purl across, increase evenly (if needed) to # of stitches for body width. Change to larger needles. For back, work in stitch pattern until 1" less than total length; for front, work in stitch pattern until 3" less than total length.

Front, round neck shaping

Because it involves a curve, this is the most difficult part of the drop shoulder garment to master. But it's not really very difficult, and we use it so often!

1. The Measurements

The first measurement you need is neck width before finishing; for most adults, I use 7½" as standard. The second measurement you need is front neck depth; before finishing, my standard for an adult is 3". You will find round necks shaped at 6" X 4" and scooped necks shaped at 9" X 2". Whichever numbers you choose, it is important that they add up to 10 to 11".

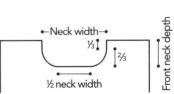

2. The Calculations

- Multiply the gauge by 7.5 = # of stitches in neck width; round up or down to an even number if the # of stitches in body width is even or to an odd number if the # of stitches in the body width is odd.

If the # of stitches in body width is even

- Divide this # by 2 to produce two even numbers. (For example, if the # were 22, I would divide by 2 and produce 10 and 12, rather than 11 and 11.)

- One even number = # of stitches put on holder for center front neck.

- Divide other even number by 2 again = # of stitches reduced at each neck edge for curve shaping.

Selvage stitches are stitches at the edge of each piece that will go into a seam allowance. If working Mattress Stitch seams (the most invisible seams), you will need these selvage stitches.

The fact that stockinette stitch rolls to the back at the sides makes it the perfect choice for selvage sts—which will automatically roll neatly into the seam allowance. Unless the garment is worked in garter stitch (which does not require selvage stitches or a seam allowance), work first and last stitch in every row (selvage stitches) in stockinette stitch: RS knit and WS purl.

Work increases and decreases in stitches next to selvage stitches but not in the selvage stitches themselves. For the neatest seams possible, the integrity of these selvage stitches must be maintained.

ROUND NECK TRIM
When picking up along a curve the following rules apply.

- **Knit sts off holder.**
- **Pick up one st for every bound-off st.**
- **Pick up one st for every "step" between bound-off sts.**
- **Pick up three sts for every four rows along a straight edge.**

When picking up around a curve, we inevitably run into holes. Do not pick up a stitch in a hole, this will simply make the hole larger; rather, close the hole by picking up a stitch in the tight spot next to it.

If the # of stitches in body width is odd

- Divide this # by 2 to produce one odd number and one even number. (For example, if the # were 23, I would divide by 2 and produce 11 and 12.)

- The odd number = # of stitches put on hold for center front neck

- Divide the even # by 2 = # of stitches reduced at each neck edge for curve shaping.

For all situations

- Multiply the row gauge by 3 = # of rows in neck depth; round up or down to an even number.

- Divide this number into 2/3 and 1/3, producing 2 even numbers. (For example, if the number were 28, I would divide into 2/3 and 1/3 and produce 18 and 10)

- 2/3 = # of rows for curve shaping.

- 1/3 = # of rows to be worked straight.

- Match # of stitches to be reduced at neck edge for curve shaping against # of rows for curve shaping.

- Because stitches to be reduced will be bound off at neck edge, divide # of rows for curve shaping by 2 = opportunities to reduce stitches at neck edge.

- Try reducing 3 stitches once, then 2 stitches once, and if there are 4–6 stitches remaining, this is fine (meaning you would bind off 3 stitches once, 2 stitches once, 1 stitch for remainder of stitches to be reduced).

- If more than 4–6 stitches remain, increase initial numbers slightly (by, for example, binding off 2 stitches more than once).

- If fewer than 4–6 stitches remain, decrease initial numbers slightly (for example, by binding off 2 stitches twice rather than 3 stitches once and 2 stitches once).

3. The Pattern
At 3" before total length, put center front neck stitches on hold. Work each side separately. Bind off stitches to be reduced at each neck edge over rows for neck shaping (for example, by binding off 3 stitches once, 2 stitches one or more times, then binding off 1 stitch 4–6 times). Work remaining rows straight to desired length.

Front, V-neck Shaping
Although less common, the V-neck is flattering for those of us with less than swan-like necks. (I have a long, skinny neck, so I didn't like this neck shaping until I learned to wear it over T-shirts or with hand-knit lace scarves.)

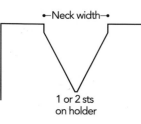

←Neck width→

Front neck depth

1 or 2 sts
on holder

1. The Measurements
The first measurement you need is unfinished neck width. Because V-neck shaping gives a larger opening than round neck shaping, it can and should be cut a little narrower: 6½" is enough.

The second measurement you need is unfinished front neck depth, and this can vary greatly. The V-neck can be drafted to plunge to the navel or to tuck tidily under the chin. One thing to keep in mind is that a 1" ribbed edge will fill in an extra ½" or more of the neck depth. Standard unfinished depth is about 8".

2. The Calculations

For a standard 8" neck depth
- Multiply the gauge by 6½" = # of stitches in neck width; round up or down to an even number if the # of stitches in body width is even; round up or down to an odd number if the # of stitches in the body width is odd.

If the # of stitches in body width is even
- Subtract 2 from this #; these 2 stitches will be left on hold at the center of the V.

If the # of stitches in body width is odd
- Subtract 1 from this #; this 1 st will be left on hold at the center of the V.

For all situations
- Divide the remaining # of neck sts by 2 = # of stitches to be reduced at each neck edge.

- Multiply the row gauge by 8 = # of rows in neck depth; round up or down to an even #.

- Divide the # of stitches to be reduced into the # of rows in neck depth; this will likely produce a fraction (for example, 3.375). Ignore the number(s) after the decimal. The # before the decimal is the rate of decrease. (For example, in this case the rate of decrease is 3, so you would decrease 1 st at neck edge every 3rd row.)

3. The Pattern

At 8" from total length, put center st(s) on hold. Work each side separately. Decrease 1 st at neck edge over rows for neck shaping according to rate of decrease as calculated. Work remaining rows straight to desired length.

Back Neck Shaping
For both round and V-neck

I did not work back neck shaping…until Lily Chin explained to me that this is why my sweaters rode back at the shoulders. (Thanks Lily!) It's only an inch, but it makes a huge difference in how your garments hang on your body.

1. The Measurements
The first measurement—neck width—is exactly the same as for the front neck shaping. The second measurement—back neck depth—is 1". (These directions are a little weird because at some point the number of stitches equals the number of rows. Just follow the steps as written and you'll "get it.")

2. The Calculations
- Round the # of rows in 1" up or down to an even number = # of rows in back neck depth.

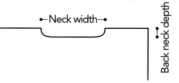

- Take this # and subtract 2; remaining # = rows for neck shaping and total # of stitches to be reduced at neck edges.

- Take # of stitches to be reduced at neck edges and subtract it from # of stitches in neck width; remaining # = # of stitches put on holder at center back neck.

- Take # of stitches to be reduced at neck edges and divide by 2 = # of stitches to be reduced at each neck edge.

V-NECK TRIM
When working trim for a V-neck pullover, the following rules apply.
- Knit st(s) off holder (at back neck and at point of V).
- Pick up sts along the diagonals at a rate that works: for example, 3 sts for 4 rows or 5 sts for 6 rows.
- Maintain the st(s) at the point of the V as RS k and WS p.
- For regular or shallow V, miter by dec one st on either side of st(s) at point of V each RS row.
- For a deep V, miter by dec one st on either side of st(s) at point of V each row.

RIBBING
Most directions say to rib on needles 2 sizes smaller. I find this is often not small enough. Reduce needle sizes until the right-side knit stitch of your ribbing is as small as the right-side knit stitch of your stockinette stitch.

If directions say to rib to a length of 4", we do but wonder why the ribbing seems to shrink. It "shrinks" because when it is stretched to the full garment width, it loses length. If you want the full 4", stretch the ribbing out on the needles to the full width of the garment before measuring.

To find the number of rib stitches that will make you a perfect cuff, wrap your bottom band ribbing around your wrist to fit snugly but still allow the hand to pass through.

3. The Pattern
At approximately 1" from total length, put center back stitches on hold.

Work each side separately. Bind off stitches to be reduced at each edge, 1 stitch at a time, over rows for neck shaping. Work remaining rows straight to desired length.

Sleeves
Although sleeves can be straight or flared, they are usually narrower at the cuff than at the upper arm.

1. The Measurements
As with all other pieces for the unfitted, drop shoulder garment, the sleeves should also be quite generous. For an adult, I rarely make an upper sleeve width less than 20" wide. Often, I will make it somewhere between 1 to 3" less than the width of the front of the garment.

Another measurement you need is the lower sleeve width—usually 8–12".

The sleeve length for a drop shoulder garment is a more complicated measurement than you might initially think. Since a drop shoulder garment can be bust measurement plus 8–18", this means that the body of the garment falls differing lengths down the sleeves.

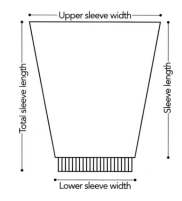

You can sort this out by doing the following: 1) find a drop shoulder garment for which the sleeve length is perfect and which has a cuff length similar to what you want to produce; 2) measure the garment from the center of the neck to the top of the cuff; 3) this number represents ½ the drop shoulder body width plus the sleeve to the cuff; 4) no matter the width of your garment, ½ its width plus sleeve length to the cuff should always add to this number.

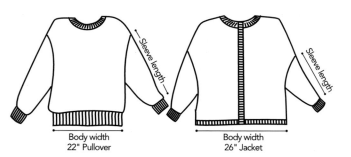

2. The Calculations
- Determine # of stitches for cuff (by wrapping bottom band around wrist so hand may slip through easily).

- Multiply the gauge by desired width at lower sleeve = # of stitches in lower sleeve.

- Add 2 selvage stitches (if doing mattress stitch seams).

- Multiply the gauge by desired width at upper sleeve = # of stitches in upper sleeve.

- Add 2 selvage stitches (if doing mattress stitch seams).

- Subtract smaller # from larger and divide by 2 = # of stitches to be increased each side of sleeve.

- Determine desired sleeve length (as described above).

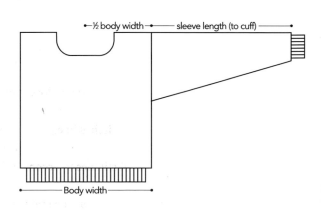

- Multiply this # by # of rows per inch = # of rows in sleeve length.

- Divide the # of stitches to be increased into the # of rows in sleeve length; this will likely produce a fraction (for example, 4.25). Ignore the number(s) after the decimal. The # before the decimal is the rate of increase (for example, in this case the rate of increase is 4, so you would increase 1 st at each edge every 4th row).

3. The Pattern

With smaller needles, cast on # of stitches for cuff; work to desired length, ending with RS row. **Next row** purl across, increasing or decreasing evenly (if needed) to # of stitches for lower sleeve width. Change to larger needles. Work in stitch pattern, centering pattern if needed, increasing 1 st each side at rate of increase as calculated, to upper sleeve width. Work straight to total sleeve length.

THE DROP SHOULDER CARDIGAN

If you think of cardigans as just pullovers with openings down the front, they become really easy to think through.

1. The Measurements

Because it opens, we assume that a cardigan will be taken on and off, and so it may be worn over other clothing. If it is not cut generously enough to look like it can do this in comfort, it may look skimpy. Therefore, for a drop shoulder cardigan which might be worn over a blouse or turtleneck, I make both the front and the back 1" wider than for a pullover—which means that my minimum finished bust measurement for a cardigan is 10" larger than my actual bust measurement. For a jacket, which might be worn over a shirt and a vest, I make it 12 to 14" larger, and for a coat, which might be worn over a sweater, up to 18" larger.

I rarely make allowance for a front edging. This means that I generally make each cardigan front just half the width of the back, plus selvages. With the edging added, this means that the front will be a little larger than the back, but this is okay: this is how we are built! If the front edging is larger than 2", however, allowances must be made: in this case, each front would be half the width of the back, minus half the width of the edging, plus selvages.

The only other measurement you need that is different from a pullover is unfinished neck width. In this case, because the garment is not pulled over the head, the neck width need not be as wide: 6–6½" is enough.

2. The Calculations

It works to figure everything out as for the pullover and then make the following changes.

- Divide body width by 2 = # of stitches in each front width

- Do you need to adjust this # of stitches to accommodate stitch pattern repeats?

- Add 2 selvage stitches (1 as selvage for side seam, 1 as selvage for front edging).

For a round neck opening

- Figure the # of stitches for neck shaping as an even number.

- Take the # of stitches that would have been put on a holder for center front neck and divide by 2 = # of stitches to be bound off at beginning of each side for neck shaping.

CARDIGAN TRIMS
I prefer cardigan bands picked up and worked out rather than knit lengthwide.
- Pick up along front edges at a rate that works: too many sts and your edging will flare, too few and it will bind.
- Practice over a 4" area of your front edge or on your gauge swatch.
- Work button bands first and sew on buttons then make buttonholes to match.

ROUND NECK
- Work the round neck trim first, picking up sts as described in the margin notes on p. 132, then work front bands.

V-NECK
- Find your proportion of sts to rows below the V: for example, 3 sts to 4 rows.
- Pick up a higher proportion of sts to rows above the V: for example, 5 sts to 6 rows.
- Pick up 3 sts at the point of V (by working k1, yo, k1 into one st).
- Failure to do these last 2 steps will produce an edging that does not lie flat—that "flips" to the front or back.

For a V-neck

- Figure the # of stitches for neck shaping as an even number (because there will be no stitch put on hold at the beginning of the neck shaping), then proceed as usual.

3. The Pattern
Work as for the pullover.

THE DROP SHOULDER PULLOVER WITH YOKE AND ROUND NECK

This shape is not much more difficult to draft than the standard drop shoulder, but it is a wonderful variation that takes that seam line off the top of the upper arm. It also works as a "frame" for the front and back pieces—for interest's sake or for when you have just enough of one yarn for the front and back and need to do the sleeves in something else. (A regular drop shoulder garment with sleeves worked in another yarn would look "stuck on," as if we really had run out of yarn! But a yoke continuing up from the sleeves is a quite different thing, and the sleeves-plus-yoke worked in another yarn look like part of a well-thought-out design.)

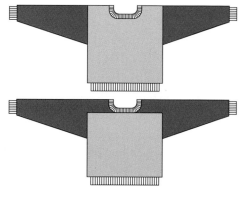

The complicating factor is that the neck shaping is worked into the sleeve yoke and, therefore, on its side.

If you remember round neck shaping, it had half its neck stitches put on a holder at the beginning of the neck shaping, then a curve was worked at each side before ending with a straight, 1" piece. The back neck had most of its stitches put on a holder and then was shaped slightly. If you turn the diagram below and to the right on its side, perhaps you can figure out how the neck is worked sideways?

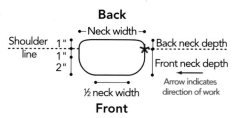

Back

← Neck width →

Shoulder line

1"
1"
2"

Back neck depth

Front neck depth

Arrow indicates direction of work

½ neck width

Front

Working in the direction of the arrow, the knitting stops at the *, and each side is worked separately. The back is shaped slightly (by binding off 2 to 3 stitches, one at a time, at each back neck edge) then worked straight. The front has 1" of stitches bound off right away, then a curve is worked (just as for the front, by binding off 2 to 3 stitches once, then 2 stitches once, then 1 stitch 4 to 6 times).

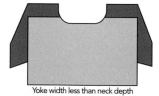
Yoke width less than neck depth

Yoke width greater than neck depth

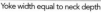

Yoke width equal to neck depth

At this point it might look as if some rows are worked straight and unshaped and then shaping is worked in reverse for the other side of the neck, but the discussion that follows (in Measurements) will explain why this is not so.

1. The Measurements

The front and back of the garment are measured and worked just as for the drop shoulder pullover except that they stop short of the total body length—by exactly half the width, or depth, of the yoke. (Look again at the sleeves with yoke diagram above. Can you see how the body length stops short and by how much?) And for this yoke width, you have three choices: less than the usual front neck depth, more than the usual front neck depth, or the same measurement as the usual front neck depth. The diagram to the left should illustrate how the latter would be the easiest to work with.

The first choice means beginning the front neck shaping in the garment, which might be a pain and certainly is not necessary. The second choice means working a strip below the front neck shaping which would need a seam in the middle or working this narrow, flimsy strip across the front of the garment. The third choice means none of the above and is actually quite simple to work!

For the third, and best, choice, the neck shaping ends after the curve is worked. The stitches that correspond to the half of the neck stitches usually put on hold at the beginning of front neck shaping will simply be picked up off the top edge of the front garment piece.

For the neck width, I take the usual 7½" and round it up to 8" (for ease of working); once you work through this pattern you may also appreciate a nice, round, easy-to-work-with number.

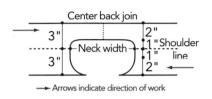

The sleeves are measured and worked just as for the drop shoulder pullover except that some portion of the center continues on to form the yoke. Since we now know that the front yoke depth is to be the same as the usual front neck depth (3"), we might as well make the back yoke depth the same, so then the entire yoke will be (6"). The length of the yoke is not a measurement but a calculation that follows.

2. The Calculations

- Make all calculations for front and back as for drop shoulder pullover except that total body length will be 3" shorter.

- Make all calculations for sleeves as for drop shoulder pullover.

- Take # of stitches in 1" and multiply by 6 = the # of stitches in yoke. Do you need to adjust this # of stitches to accommodate stitch pattern repeats?

- Add 2 selvage stitches.

- Take the # of stitches in upper sleeve width, subtract the # of stitches in yoke width, then divide by 2 = the # of stitches to be bound off each side for the end of sleeve and beginning of the yoke.

- Determine # of inches in ½ body width and subtract 4" = length of yoke to beginning of neck shaping.

3. The Pattern

Work the front and back as for the drop shoulder pullover, but bind off all stitches three inches short of total length. (These stitches could all be left on hold if you prefer to graft the yoke to the body rather than seam it.)

Work the sleeves as for the drop shoulder pullover, but at total sleeve length bind off stitches at beginning of next 2 rows, leaving only yoke-width # of stitches.

Work yoke straight to beginning of neck shaping, then work each side separately. For front neck shaping, bind off 1" of stitches at first neck edge, then 3 or 2 stitches at next neck edge, then 2 stitches at next neck edge, then 1 stitch at each following neck edge (4 to 6 times) until there are no stitches. For back neck shaping, bind off 1 stitch at beginning of next 2 to 3 neck edges, then work straight to 4" from beginning of neck shaping; put remaining stitches on holder. Work second sleeve and reverse neck shaping.

For seaming, front yoke neck shaping should end approximately 2" from center of front garment piece. As mentioned earlier, stitches for center of front neck are picked up from front garment piece. Back yoke pieces will be grafted together at center back.

RESIZING
If you've not knit to gauge, block the piece before working neck shaping.

If it is a little too large, can you call it the front (because we can all use a little extra width there), and work front neck shaping in it? If so, knit the back on fewer stitches. "Bury" the extra sts of the front in the shoulder seams and neck.

If the piece is a little too small, call it the back and make the front larger. "Bury" the extra sts of the front in the shoulder seams and neck.

Appendix

ABBREVIATIONS

approx approximate(ly)
beg begin(ning)(s)
CC contrasting color
cn cable needle
cm centimeter(s)
cont continu(e)(ed)(es)(ing)
dec decreas(e)(ed)(es)(ing)
dpn double pointed
  needle(s)
foll follow(s)(ing)
g gram(s)
" inch(es)
' foot(feet)
inc increas(e)(ed)(es)(ing)
k knit(ting)(s)(ted)
lb pound(s)
m meter(s)
mm millimeter(s)
MC main color
oz ounce(s)
p purl(ed)(ing)(s)
pat(s) pattern(s)
pm place marker
psso pass slipped
  stitch(es) over
rem remain(s)(ing)
rep repeat(s)
rev reverse(d)
RS right side(s)
rnd round(s)
sl slip(ped)(ping)
SSK slip, slip, knit 2tog
st(s) stitch(es)
St st stockinette stitch
tog together
WS wrong side(s)
wyif with yarn in front
yd yard(s)
yo yarn over

138

GRAFTING

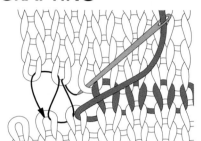

Grafting joins two pieces of knitting by working a row of knitting with tapestry needle and yarn.

1 Remove needles and stitch holder, and block pieces.
2 Arrange pieces as shown in diagram. What you will see are live stitches on both upper and lower pieces.
3 Thread blunt needle with matching yarn. (In diagram, grafting yarn is darker.)
4 Work from right to left throughout, matching gauge as closely as possible.
5 Bring yarn from back to front through first stitch on lower piece.
6 Bring yarn from back to front through first stich on upper piece.
7 **On lower piece:** bring yarn from front to back through first stitch then from back to front through next stitch.
8 **On upper piece:** bring yarn from front to back through first stitch then from back to front through next stitch.
9 **On lower piece:** bring yarn from front to back through previous stitch worked then from back to front through next stitch.
10 **On upper piece:** bring yarn from front to back through previous stitch worked then from back to front through next stitch.
11 Repeat steps 9 and 10 across.

There are five garments in this book for which grafting is suggested. For Laurel's Jacket and The Kilim Coat Dress, grafting joins the back yoke pieces seamlessly where bound-off edges turned into seam allowances would be irritating to the body. For Laurel's Jacket, the pieces are knit in stockinette stitch so a grafted join worked as above should be invisible. For the ribbed pieces of The Kilim Coat Dress and the garter stitch in Homer's Vest (where the center fronts are grafted together), this join will not be invisible. Pull the grafting tight to produce a seam with no seam allowance.

For The Inspired-by-the-Log-Cabin Jacket, grafting joins the live stitches of one piece to the side garter ridges of another, or joins a cast-on edge of one piece to the side garter ridges of another. For both, work as before but with the following differences:

1 when grafting from a cast-on edge, work through the stitches just above the cast-on edge as if they were live stitches: the cast-on edge will go into the seam allowance;
2 pick up or catch one garter ridge each time;
3 pull thread taut, pulling pieces together as you go.

For Caddy's Cardigan, both versions, grafting is used to join the live stitches at the shoulders or upper sleeves to the rolled trim. Work as before but with the following differences:

1 graft live stitches to a row of the reverse stockinette stitch edging by treating one ridge of the edging as if it were a row of live stitches;
2 pull thread taut, pulling pieces together as you go.

CROCHET CAST-ON

1 Make slip knot on crochet hook. Hold crochet hook in right hand and knitting needle on top of yarn in left hand. With hook to right of yarn, bring yarn through loop on hook; yarn goes over top of needle forming a stitch.
2 *Bring yarn under point of needle and hook yarn over needle and through loop forming next stitch; repeat from* to last stitch.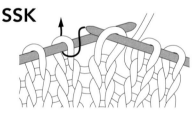
2 Bring yarn under point of needle and slip loop from hook to needle for last stitch.

SSK

1. Slip 2 stitches one at a time to right needle, slipping as if to knit.

2. Knit these 2 stitches together by slipping left hand needle from left to right through the front of both stitches.

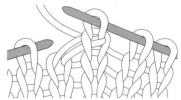

3. Knit 2 together with right hand needle.

SEWING & CUTTING

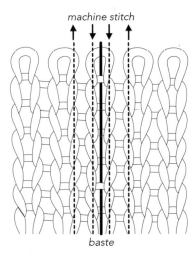

machine stitch

baste

1   Baste with a contrasting color yarn exactly where you want to cut. Keep most of the basting on top so it shows.
2   Machine stitch using the smallest straight stitch you can. Stitch down the ridge formed by the stitches closest to the basting on one side and back up the ridge next to it. Repeat on the other side of the basting line.
3   Check to see that the stitching is in the right place. Note for the faint-hearted: Secure from fraying by soaking the cutting line with a product called "Fray Check" (available at fabric stores). It smells awful, dries hard, but washes soft. Let it dry completely before cutting.
4   Cut on the basting yarn.

In the patterns, a reverse stockinette stitch edging is worked and wraps around and covers the rough cut edges.

CIRCULAR FAIRISLE

For the body of fairisle cardigans worked circularly,

1   work color changes at front opening,
2   do not bother to weave-in ends,
3   before sewing and cutting, pull ends taut and secure and hold them out of the way with a piece of tape.

Before cutting, it's also a good idea to wash or block the pieces so the stitches are "set".

GARTER RIDGE JOINS

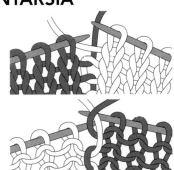

Pieces worked in garter stitch seam quite simply and as follows.

1   Block pieces.
2   Arrange pieces as shown in diagram.
3   Thread blunt needle with yarn to match garment. (In diagram, seaming yarn is darker.)
4   Pick up or catch a garter ridge from one piece as shown in diagram.
5   Cross to matching place on opposite piece and pick up or catch one garter ridge.
6   Pull thread taut, pulling pieces together as you go.

DUPLICATE STITCH

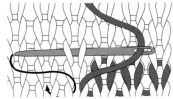

Duplicate stitch (also known as Swiss darning) is just that: with a blunt tapestry needle threaded with contrast color yarn, cover a knit stitch with an embroidered stitch of the same shape.

INTARSIA

When changing from one color to the next when working intarsia, it is necessary to twist the yarns to prevent holes.
Pick up the new color from under the old color, as shown, and continue working.

3-ROW BUTTONHOLE

This buttonhole opening runs perpendicular to the rows of the band.
In k1, p1 (k2, p2) rib:
Row 1 (RS) Work to k1 (2nd k of k2), SSK, yo twice.
Row 2 Work to yo's, drop one yo and k into back of remaining yo.
Row 3 Work to yo-stitch, p through space below, drop yo stitch from left hand needle.

METRICS
To convert inches to centimeters, multiply the inches by 2.5.
For example:
4" x 2.5 = 10cm

To convert feet to centimeters, multiply the feet by 30.48.
For example:
2' x 30.48 = 60.96cm

To convert yards to meters, multiply the yards by .9144.
For example:
4 yds x .9144 = 3.66m

MATTRESS STITCH

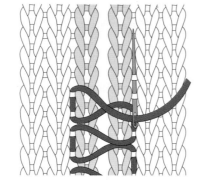

Mattress stitch seams are quite invisible. They require selvage stitches (which are taken into the seam allowance) and are worked with right side facing.
The process is as follows.

1   Block pieces.
2   Arrange pieces as shown in diagram.
3   Thread blunt needle with yarn to match garment. (In diagram, seaming yarn is darker.)
4   Working between selvage stitch and next stitch (in diagram, selvage stitch is darker), pick up 2 bars.
5   Cross to matching place in opposite piece, and pick up 2 bars.
6   Return to first piece, go down into the hole you came out of, and pick up 2 bars.
7   Return to opposite piece, go down into the hole you came out of, and pick up 2 bars.
8   Repeat steps 6 and 7 across, pulling thread taut as you go.

Note For Knitting as Warp fabric pieces, pick up only 1 bar at a time. These instructions are for seaming side or underarm seams. When seaming shoulders, use the same process but with the following differences:

1   treat the bound-off edges as selvage stitches;
2   pick up 1 stitch each time instead of 2 bars.

When seaming upper sleeves to body, use the same process but with the following differences:

1   treat the bound-off edge of the upper sleeve as selvage stitch;
2   pick up stitches along upper sleeve instead of bars;
3   to prevent puckering of either fabric, pick up 1 bar instead of 2 or ½ stitch instead of 1, as required.

LIFTED INCREASE

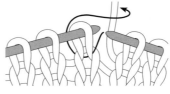

1   Knit into the purl bump behind the next st on the left-hand needle.

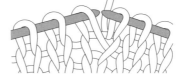

2   Completed lifted increase. Knit the next stitch and continue.
3   **On wrong side rows,** purl into the purl bump in front of the next stitch on the left hand needle.

WEAVING IN ENDS

Tail ends should be woven-in over 8–10 sts. Weave beginning tails over the next row worked in the same direction. Weave ending tails over the next row. This is easiest when the working yarn is in the right hand and the tail end is in the left.
Bring the tail end yarn over right needle and knit a stitch, being careful not to knit the tail. Slip tail end off needle and knit next stitch. Repeat from.

SINGLE CROCHET

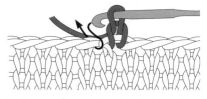

1   Insert the crochet hook into the fabric, catch the yarn and pull up a loop. Bring yarn over hook through loop on hook.

2   *Insert hook into next stitch and pull up a loop.

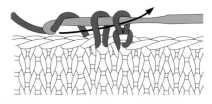

3   Yarn over and through both loops on hook—one single crochet (sc). Rep from*.

LATCHING

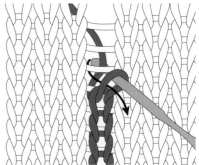

Latching is used in Shannon's Pullover to fill holes produced in weaving. With crochet hook at front of work and yarn at back, latch one chain stitch in each space up vertical line between color blocks.

The color wheel

These color wheels can help you see the pattern your color choices produce.

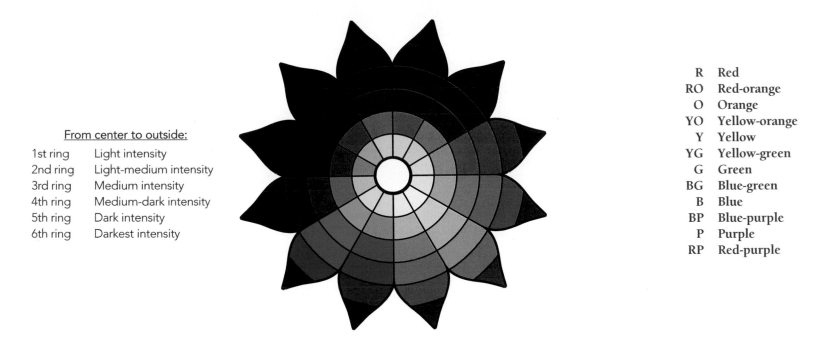

From center to outside:

1st ring	Light intensity
2nd ring	Light-medium intensity
3rd ring	Medium intensity
4th ring	Medium-dark intensity
5th ring	Dark intensity
6th ring	Darkest intensity

R	Red
RO	Red-orange
O	Orange
YO	Yellow-orange
Y	Yellow
YG	Yellow-green
G	Green
BG	Blue-green
B	Blue
BP	Blue-purple
P	Purple
RP	Red-purple

Match your yarns to the colors on the full intensity wheel…

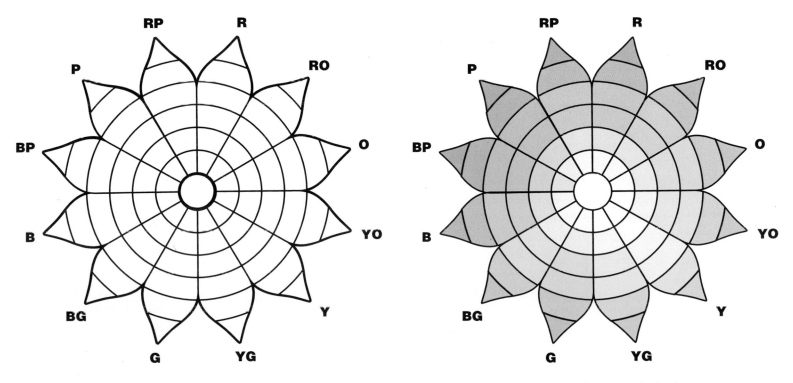

…then mark these by outlining or by filling in with colored pencil on a photocopy of the ghosted wheel.

Colophon

DAVE MINNES

Scenic Waterloo County, Ontario, Canada, was the backdrop for Sally Melville Styles: (THIS PAGE) Sally and the XRX editorial team—Mark Sampson, Nancy J. Thomas, Elaine Rowley, and Alexis Xenakis with modeling student Homer in Rockwood Provincial Park. (OPPOSITE PAGE) The Minnes Family—Dave, Sandi, Jonathan, and Kevin; West Montrose covered bridge and environs; and the quaint town of Elora.

"The places that Sally found for us to photograph were just magical," says *Sally Melville Styles* Fashion Director Nancy J. Thomas. "With such delightful surroundings, I felt like we were on a holiday rather than on a busy shoot."

The backdrop for *Sally Melville Styles* was Sally's backyard, scenic Waterloo County, Ontario. Our crew included Nancy, Sally, her daughter Caddy, beloved miniature schnauzer Homer (who made his modeling debut), XRX Books Editor Elaine Rowley, then-XRX-Art-Director Mark Sampson, and Sally's friends the Minnes family: Sandi, Jonathan, and Kevin who stood good naturedly in front of our camera, and Dave behind it—he's responsible for two of the photos on these pages.

"We spent an uncharacteristically chilly but sunny May 24th weekend photographing in the Elora Quarry and Gorge, the West Montrose covered bridge, the farm fields outside Breslau, the grassy park lands near my home, and in Rockwood Provincial Park," Sally says. "Amidst the wind, clouds, water, it was a hectic, intense, wonderful time—it was like a picnic. And I love that my garments are shown against my landscape!"

The garments in *Sally Melville Styles* were five years in the making. "My teenage daughter Caddy had asked me to knit a sweater for her boyfriend," Sally explains. "There's always the risk that at that age the boyfriend is going to be out of the picture by the time the sweater is finished, so you don't want to spend a lot of money on the yarn—you want to enjoy the knitting, make something nice for someone special, but not put cash on the line!

"This was Topher's Pullover, the first tweed stitch squares garment. I was about half-way through the back

and it was progressing beautifully. I had taken on full-time work—as Study Skills Advisor at a large Canadian University—and the job was being offered to me on a permanent basis. But I didn't feel it was the best time to be working full-time: my husband had died the year before, and I had two teenagers still at home.

"If I severely cut back my hours at the university, how would I fill my time? I looked down at this beautiful sweater I was knitting and thought, 'I will write a book about using up leftovers!'

"And this is the true story about the moment this book began: not as a deliberate, market-driven project, but as a solution to a simple, rather mundane, problem.

"To proceed, I ventured four ways. One was to continue developing tweed stitch squares (chapters 4 and 5). Another was to look at garments I had already worked from my stash and to re-develop them (chapters 2 and 3). One, the brown version of Laurel's Jacket, was made from very expensive leftovers. The first time I wore it, a woman said, 'That is the most beautiful garment I have

ever seen.' My response was a very inconsiderate exclamation: 'You're kidding! It's made out of leftovers!' This was my first "eureka" moment with respect to leftovers—that they could produce beautiful fabrics!

The other two explorations happened simultaneously: what could I do with our simplest stitch patterns, and what new technique could I develop? The Good Ol' Garter section (chapter 1) is my response to the former, and the Knitting as Warp section (chapter 6) is my response to the latter.

"Toward the middle of those five years, I began to seriously pursue a publisher. It was a wonderful thing that I found my place with XRX."

By the time *Sally Melville Styles* entered production, Mark had designed the cover and moved west. The job of designing the book fell to Bob Natz, a graphic artist of rare talent with whom we worked on our very first issue of *Knitter's*. "The book came together quite comfortably with the four necessary ingredients," Bob says. "A unique knitting concept; beautiful photographs of beautiful fabrics; a color system that complements both; and a wonderfully written dialog.

"I wanted the book design to showcase the photography and other graphic elements while not getting in the way of concentration and enjoyment. And I chose typefaces that enhanced the design while allowing for easy readability: ITC Berkeley Oldstyle for the body type, because it has a complete set of faces and is a very readable typestyle and Albertus MT for the headlines because of its texture and direct contrast to the Berkeley."

Bob's design was implemented on Macintosh PowerPC computers using QuarkXPress™ and Adobe Illustrator™. Adobe Photoshop™ and digital separations allowed unparalleled color control: we were fortunate to have Publishing Services Director David Xenakis (a knitter and co-author with knitter Sherry London of *Photoshop 5 in Depth* (Coriolis Group). Using color-adjusted work stations, David and Digital Color Specialist Daren Morgan precisely matched color files to Sally's sweaters. Xaos Tools' Terrazzo 2™ (an Adobe Photoshop add on) allowed a kaleidoscopic digital presentation of Sally's color mixing strategy (page 17).

Book Production Manager Debbie Gage brought it all together in digital page color layouts printed on an Epson Rip Station 5000™ ink-jet printer. These files were converted to Adobe Acrobat™ documents that, through the magic of the Internet, were accessible to Editor Elaine Rowley's Power Macintosh in Sioux Falls, and author Sally Melville's Windows PC in Canada as downloadable files from our transfer site.

DAVE MINNES

Webmaster Benjamin Xenakis made sure none of us got stranded on the information superhighway.

From Sally's needles, my Hasselblad, and our XRX team we present *Sally Melville Styles*.

—Alexis Yiórgos Xenakis
Sioux Falls, South Dakota

other publications from XRX, Inc.

Magnificent Mittens
Anna Zilboorg

Ethnic Socks and Stockings
Priscilla A. Gibson-Roberts

The Great American Afghan

Knitter's Magazine

Weaver's Magazine

BOOKS

144